GUIDED BY GRACE

MY JOURNEY OF SPIRITUAL AWAKENING AND STEPS TO PERSONAL FREEDOM

NOOR AKHTER

About the Author

Noor Akhter lives in the UK with her three children. She has faced many challenges in life, which have led to a journey of spiritual awakening, healing, and self-discovery. Following her awakening, Noor underwent a major transformation. "Guided by Grace" is her autobiography, chronicling a journey of resilience and finding strength in the face of adversity. Noor plans to write more books on personal growth, with her next book focusing on women's empowerment, coming soon.

Noor's sole purpose is to aid in humanity's healing and soul evolution, allowing us to live lives filled with ease and abundance. She works as a spiritual life coach, helping others with her intuitive, transformational, and empathetic coaching style. Noor's special coaching skills include healing from narcissistic abuse, overcoming co-dependency, relationship and parenting skills, and manifesting love and abundance.

Dedication

I dedicate this book to my son, Raham Ahmed. Thank you for teaching me important life lessons by being authentic, resilient, and honest to your true self and soul essence. Words cannot describe how much I love you.

Thank you to my sons Aneeq and Talal. Your presence in my life gives me the courage to keep going no matter what. You bring purpose and joy to my life, and being a mom to my three kids is the best thing that has ever happened to me.

Thank you to all the souls who have come into my life and crossed my path for your blessings and lessons.

Thank you to the NHS staff at LGI Hospital in Leeds for giving my son Raham the best care.

Acknowledgments

This book came into being almost by itself in my mind, but to bring it into physical reality, I would like to express my deepest gratitude to all those who supported me throughout its creation, especially my editor Dianne, and Michelle and Hira, for their great efforts, feedback, and guidance during the writing process.

Huge thanks to my kids for their patience and understanding, and for being enthusiastic about my book.

Thanks to my niece, Aqsa Shaukat, for her love, support, and belief in me. A huge thanks to my lovely clients who shared their stories with me. Thank you for trusting me and inspiring me to write this book.

Although my journey has been almost solo, I believe I received a lot of help from Source, spirit guides, and angels. So, thanks to God and my spirit team.

Finally, I would like to express my deep appreciation to myself, for choosing struggles and hardships for growth over comfort, for not dimming your light for others, for standing with your authentic true self, and for not compromising your values, dignity, and self-respect. Thank you for listening to your higher self and writing this book.

TABLE OF CONTENTS

Introduction

"What happens in your life is not 100% in your control. But what you make of it is 100% up to you." - Sadhguru

Before my spiritual awakening, I used to think I was the only person on this planet who was suffering, and that I was the only one with such an abusive mother. I was a very reserved person and never talked or shared with anyone about my struggles and the mental torture and abuse from my mother. Because I did not share my struggles, people did not share theirs with me, and I struggled to connect with others.

As soon as I started opening up, people began to open up to me easily. Because I am a hairdresser, I meet many women every day. Due to my empathetic nature, being a good listener, and being nonjudgmental, my clients feel comfortable sharing their stories, traumas, and struggles with me. I realised it is not just me who has struggled in life; we all go through different kinds of struggles, hardships, and traumas.

Some of my clients' stories were more traumatic than mine, which touched my heart deeply. I feel immense compassion for people who have been through traumas and abuse. I found out that there are billions of people on this planet who are suffering. Struggle, pain, and suffering are inevitable. We cannot avoid them by denying, resisting, or running from them.

As struggle and suffering are a part of life, what we do with them is entirely up to us. We can choose to be stuck in a victim mentality, or we can transcend our trials and struggles for our personal growth, evolution, and freedom. The reason I am sharing my story with the world is to inspire others and let them know that no matter how traumatised we are and how many hardships we must face, there is always a possibility for healing, growth, and transformation.

From my personal experience, I can certainly say that there is no wound you cannot heal, no person you cannot forgive, and no

1

darkness where light cannot reach. Living your life in an asleep state with your shadows is living in darkness; our consciousness is light. Darkness is the absence of light. As soon as we let the light of our consciousness touch our being, darkness will start disappearing.

It might take a few or many years, depending on the person, but the light will help you see your shadows so you can transcend them. It takes time because when we get used to living in an asleep state and darkness for lifetimes and years upon years, waking up to light suddenly and seeing all our blind spots and shadows at once can be overwhelming. It's like if a person whose eyes are used to darkness for many years suddenly has a 1000-volt bulb turned on. They will not be able to open their eyes, or it might hurt their eyes.

The same happens when our consciousness starts awakening. Our soul and guides know all our shadows, blind spots, beliefs, and energetic blocks. They show us our shadows at a speed we can handle, but only if we allow them and ourselves to see.

One important law of the universe is the law of free will. Although we are never alone and do have help from the spirit realm, including angels, spirit guides, and our higher selves, which is our soul, they never force us to heal unless we allow it or have soul contracts with them, which we made before even coming to this earth. Sometimes our physical mind may not allow it, but our higher selves can give permission for healing.

We live in a supportive, loving, and abundant universe. How we use that support for our highest good is up to us. Seeing our own wounds, flaws, shadows, and blind spots may look frightening, but if we choose to see ourselves and others without judgment and with compassion, the self-discovery journey can be exciting. I am not saying it will be easy, but it will be an adventure with many highs and lows for brave souls.

Thank you for holding my book in your hands. May reading this book bring light into your life and show you the ways to connect to your own inner healer, higher self, and guides. I wish you the best of luck on your healing journey.

Special Note

In this book, I have changed the real names of people to respect their privacy. However, my children's names, my niece's name, and my best friend's name are real.

Noor Akhter

Chapter 1: Roots of Resilience

I come from a small village in Punjab, Pakistan, but most of my life played out in Lahore. I'm the seventh in a brood of nine – four older brothers, two sisters older than me, and a younger brother and sister. Life was tough, to say the least.

Our home, tucked away in a Lahore slum, saw us through childhood and teenage years steeped in poverty. Our meals were simple, usually just vegetable curry and roti (naan bread). Fancy things like fruits and meat were rare treats, saved for special occasions. My dad, once a farmer in Naruwal, switched to labor jobs when we moved to Lahore. Both my parents lacked formal education but worked hard to get by.

Life took a turn when my elder brother got divorced. His two kids, Aqsa and her brother, came to live with us. Meanwhile, my two elder sisters got married and moved away, leaving me to navigate these early years.

Money, or the lack of it, became a constant source of tension at home. My mom, tightly holding onto money matters, clashed with my dad and brothers regularly. Their fights echoed through our home, shattering any hope of peace.

My dad, not one to be abusive, kept to himself, finding refuge in his work. But my mom, struggling with her mental health, unleashed both mental and physical pain on us, especially my brothers. Her battles were loud, relentless, and lasted for what felt like forever. Our house, instead of being a haven, turned into a war zone.

My mom's control extended to every aspect of our lives. She wouldn't let us talk, laugh, or spend time together. We became strangers in our own home, living side by side but disconnected, drowned in fear.

Our home was a chilling tapestry of fear and chaos. The battles we fought within our family mirrored the harsh realities of the world outside. It's a story etched in my heart, one that brings tears when I look back.

In the world where I grew up, being keen on studies and loving books made me stand out, especially in Pakistan where reading wasn't very common among kids. My little haven was a trunk filled with children's books, bought with the pocket money my dad generously gave me.

I vividly recall a summer afternoon when I was about 5, lost in the pages of a storybook. The house was unusually peaceful – a rare occurrence when my mom was away. We loved those moments of quiet when her absence allowed us to relax and breathe a little easier. However, the tranquility shattered when she stormed into the room, anger etched on her face. In an instant, my book was taken away, and a stinging slap marked my cheek. Her anger continued as she took it all out on my siblings.

Left alone in my room, tears streamed down my face, a mixture of shock and sadness. Despite my older sibling being at home, there was no comforting presence, no one to ask how I was doing. Fear gripped me, preventing me from crying aloud, afraid that my mom might be triggered to slap me again.

In that moment, I instinctively built a strong shield around me, a coping mechanism to numb the overwhelming emotions. My world, limited to the school and the walls of our home, lacked exposure to the outer world. And who would even come to our house? My mom's behavioral issues severed ties with my entire extended family, and her difficulty getting along with neighbors left us as a somewhat isolated family. We were broken and alone. People were afraid to even interact with us, lest my mother gets to know of it. And then what? I used to wonder. There were seven billion people in the world, my teacher told me, and yet I felt terribly alone. I was afraid to speak in front of my mom. I missed my own voice sometimes. Standing in front of the mirror, I saw a child with pale shrunken cheeks. The weight of our collective isolation was too heavy. It was a burden of unspoken pain.

When I was a kid, our house was a tough place. There were fights, and I'd hide in a room, praying with all my heart for God to make it stop. I'd pray for hours until the fights quieted down. Even though the fights didn't stop right away, those prayers helped me feel close to God. It was like a little bit of peace in the middle of all the chaos.

I felt kind of invisible at home. My mom had money problems, and in our culture, people mostly focus on the guys in the family. Even though my mom was busy with my brothers, she'd still be really strict and mean to me. My older sibling couldn't go to school, but I went to a government school where we sat on the floor. It wasn't until I was in the fifth year that I got a chair. English classes started in the sixth year. Going to school was my safe place, away from the troubles at home, even if just for a little while each day.

So, growing up was hard. I'd pray to God in that little room, finding comfort in believing He was watching over me. School became my escape, a place where I could forget about everything happening at home. It's tough looking back, but those prayers and the time at school kept me going, even when things were really sad.

At 13, my world crumbled when my dad passed away. A few months later, I found my mom in a tearful argument with my older brother, pleading with him to work and bring in some money. The pain in her voice and the tears on her cheeks were like a storm cloud over our home.

Driven by a child's belief that money could fix everything, I went to my mom, offering comfort. Placing my hand on her head, I promised, "Mom, I'll work and earn money for you." It seemed straightforward to my 13-year-old mind – solve the money problem, make Mom happy.

So, during summer break, I started learning hair and beauty at a local salon. Even when school started, I kept going after classes. After a year of learning, I landed a full-time job at another salon.

When I finally handed my first paycheck to Mom, she was taken aback. Holding those four thousand rupees, her overwhelmed happiness overflowed into kissing the money notes. But the joy didn't extend to me. No appreciation or acknowledgment came my way.

Even my younger sister, witnessing it all, urged Mom to recognize the effort. "Mom, you should kiss your daughter who earned the money," she said. Yet, Mom seemed deaf to those words and blind to what I had done.

In that moment, the realisation hit me – no amount of money could bridge the gap or bring the appreciation I sought. It became clear that pleasing Mom was an impossible task, and the innocence of my 13-year-old self-shattered like fragile glass.

Every day, getting to the salons where I worked was like a tough adventure. I had to take two or sometimes three buses, and it was far from my home. This journey, from home to work and back, using public transport, was especially hard for a teenage girl in Pakistan. Girls usually don't travel alone there because it's not very safe.

Men on the buses would stare at me, say different names, and some even tried to touch me inappropriately. It made me feel really uncomfortable and scared. But even with all that, I still found the courage to go to work every day.

Even though I was scared, I kept going. Each trip became a small victory against the fear that tried to hold me back. The journey to work turned into a kind of silent rebellion, where I faced discomfort and fear but still pushed ahead.

There is one memory that always haunts me whenever I think about it. That one time that I almost got saved. Almost. The word almost has such a painful ring to it. It can change your life in a jiffy. I could have been almost raped. Almost abused. Almost traumatized. Almost dead. Almost. I hate it, and yet it is the reality of so many women in Pakistan. I was lucky, and yet I hate the word being associated with me, because what if I hadn't been lucky? What if someone is not lucky, and is in a bad situation at a bad time? It's not their fault. I hate being vigilant at all times, but that was my reality. I had to stay alert, I was a prey and the predators were at loose.

Life was not fair. I had to work at a very young age, I had to earn money, I had to ward off the evil eyes of men, and go home and suffer the mental abuse at the hands of my mother. What a life.

In the middle of my full-time job, I clung to my studies like a lifeline. The weight of my mother's constant mental and psychological abuse had made my three elder brothers incapable of contributing to the family's financial well-being. It was a burden we, my only working elder brother Adil and I, shouldered alone.

While I juggled work and education, my younger sister and brother were still in the tender years of childhood, studying. Our combined incomes, from my meager earnings and Adil's salary, were just enough to scrape by. It was a delicate balance, where every rupee counted, ensuring that the ends met, if only just.

Yet, in the midst of this financial struggle, the storms within our home refused to go away. My mother's rage, her abuse, the loud shouting, and our fights stayed in the air like a heavy storm. The very walls of our home seemed to absorb the pain, becoming silent witnesses to the chaos that refused to decrease.

Each day, the weight of our responsibilities bore down on us, threatening to crush the stability we had established. In the heart of our efforts to make ends meet, the emotional toll was immeasurable. Our lives felt like a sad song, a mix of strength and struggle against the tough times we faced. It wasn't just about money; our home was a constant battleground of emotions. We tried hard to make things work, but the chaos at home made it tough.

When I was 21 years old, word got around that there was a salon up for sale. Now, I didn't exactly have stacks of cash lying around, but the idea intrigued me. So, I convinced my mom to accompany me to check out the salon and have a chat with the dealer.

At first, my mom was hesitant. She reminded me that we didn't have the funds for such an investment, and she doubted we ever would. Despite her discouragement, I was determined. So, I turned to my sister-in-law and asked her to join me on this venture.

Together, we went to see the salon and spoke with the dealer. The place had potential, and I could feel my excitement growing with each passing moment. But then came the hefty price tag – 150,000 PKR, a sum that felt like a mountain to us back in 2004.

That's when I turned to my sister-in-law with a proposition. She had gold jewelry, so I proposed a partnership. I asked her to invest 75,000 PKR by selling her jewelry, and in return, I promised her a 50% share of the business profits. To my relief and joy, she agreed wholeheartedly.

Back when I was working in another salon, I had the pleasure of working under the ownership of a lady named Nisa. Even though my time there was short, I had formed a good rapport with her. Nisa, an American citizen, eventually sold her salon and returned to the States. However, before leaving, she entrusted me with her landline number. Despite the distance and lack of regular contact, when I found myself in need of funds to pursue my own salon dreams, I mustered up the courage to reach out to her.

It was a leap of faith, really. Nisa and I hadn't spoken since she left, and she wasn't even aware of my current address. But to my surprise and gratitude, she readily agreed to lend me the 75 thousand rupees I needed. I repaid her in installments, as agreed upon, with the help of a friend she had in Pakistan. Though our direct contact dwindled thereafter, I will forever cherish her generosity and trust – it truly felt like a miracle.

Fast forward to the time when my youngest sister completed her high school education and joined me in our very own salon venture. Our salon, though modest, was nestled not too far from our home. Business began to pick up, and in the first year alone, I found myself making ten times more than what I used to earn as an employee in someone else's salon. It was a gratifying feeling to know that a portion of those profits was going back to my brother's household. He, like me, was one of the few hard workers in our family, toiling away as a laborer in a factory. His earnings were hardly enough to provide for his young daughters, so I was glad to be able to contribute.

To make our daily commute easier, my brother Adil began giving my sister and me lifts on his bike after our shifts. In the mornings, we'd hop into a rickshaw to get to work. It was a small gesture, but it made a world of difference. During this time, I also managed to earn my bachelor's degree, adding another achievement to my list of accomplishments.

As our lifestyle gradually improved, we experienced prosperity in our household for the first time. My routine was simple – I would hand over my earnings to my mom after taking my pocket money. However, one morning, things took an unexpected turn. My sister and I were getting ready for work when, without any apparent reason, my mom started shouting at us. Hastily, we prepared ourselves, eager to escape her mental torment, or at least made an attempt. As we left the house and made our way towards the main road to catch a rickshaw to the salon, my mom trailed behind us, hurling insults and expletives until we were seated in the rickshaw. Throughout the ordeal, my sister and I remained silent, feeling embarrassed and frightened, like scared children. For me, every abusive insult hurled towards me since I was a child flashed in front of me, pulling me back to the gloom I thought I had left behind. That fifteen-minute walk felt like an eternity, a painful reminder of the emotional wounds inflicted by our own mother. Sadly, this wasn't an isolated incident – it happened frequently. Sometimes, my mom would follow us all the way to the salon, continuing her tirade even inside the premises, that would lead to my customers gawking at us, regret of coming there in the first place evident in their eyes.

Despite being adults, my sister and I were emotionally battered by our mother's relentless abuse, rendering us unable to defend ourselves. Whenever she unleashed her verbal onslaught, it felt as though her words were daggers piercing through our minds. To shield ourselves from the onslaught, we would instinctively cover our ears with our hands, but that would not make a difference. As every single cell in our bodies were very much aware of what words were being barked out of her mouth.

Eventually, circumstances led to my three brothers going their separate ways, leaving my mom, my elder brother with his two kids, my younger sibling, and me under one roof. At home, I felt like a frightened child, much like my other siblings. However, my skills in the salon were flourishing, and the business was growing. Yet, even there, I encountered challenges. My younger sister, inheriting my mom's traits, made my work life difficult. Despite being five years my junior, she harbored intense jealousy towards me due to my experience. Unable to confront me directly, she resorted to throwing tantrums and emanating negative energy.

Despite contemplating moving out and living in a girls' hostel to escape the toxic environment at home, I couldn't bring myself to abandon my younger brother, sister, and my elder brother's children. I was their only emotional support, especially considering my elder brother's lack of employment. Financially, I shouldered the responsibility of supporting my niece, Aqsa, and nephew. They held a special place in my heart, particularly because they lacked a mother figure. My mom, however, viewed them as burdens, often picking fights with my brother over the kids and subjecting them to further abuse. In this tumultuous household, Aqsa was the only one I felt close to. Despite the challenges, she continued her studies as I established my own salon.

My niece Aqsa, just a teenager at the time, found herself on my mom's radar for torture. Despite shouldering the burden of household chores alongside her studies, Aqsa endured relentless abuse from my mom. It was heart-wrenching to hear her recount how my mom would shout, yell, and often physically assault her. Aqsa bore the brunt of my mom's anger more than anyone else, and I couldn't help but feel a deep sense of sorrow for her plight. Unfortunately, Aqsa's father, my elder brother, was emotionally weak and unemployed, unable to shield his own daughter from his mother's wrath.

One particular incident stands out in my memory. On the day of Aqsa's exam, my mom erupted in a fit of rage, slapping her across the face and locking her in her room to prevent her from attending the exam. It was a cruel tactic, exploiting Aqsa's vulnerability and love for her studies. That day, I summoned the courage I never knew I had. I intervened, unlocking the door and standing between my mom and Aqsa, determined to put an end to her suffering. The sight of Aqsa's tear-streaked face filled me with a profound sadness and helplessness, yet fueled my resolve to protect her.

In a moment of defiance, I packed our belongings and informed my mom that Aqsa and I were leaving the house. Despite her initial shock, my mom continued to berate Aqsa, shifting blame onto her for the situation. Desperate to escape, I was resolute in my decision, until my sister-in-law, who shared a partnership with me in the salon, intervened. Witnessing the turmoil, she persuaded me to reconsider, and out of respect for her, we reluctantly stayed.

Returning to the salon that day, my heart weighed heavy with the knowledge that Aqsa remained at home with my mom. I couldn't shake the feeling of guilt and unease, but for the time being, I had no other choice.

Recognizing that my mom suffered from mental health issues, I sought help for her. I took her to see a psychiatrist, who prescribed medication. However, my mom refused to take the medication, citing its sedative effects, which interfered with her desire to avoid excessive sleep. Despite my efforts, she adamantly refused to see the doctor again, leaving me feeling utterly helpless in the face of her stubborn resistance. Something had to be done, but what… that I had to figure out.

Chapter 2 – Tangled Vows

When I was working as an employee at Madam Nisa's salon, I met Nafees there. He had an advertising agency. Madam Nisa used to place ads for the salon through his agency. I was 19 years old at the time, and he was 22 years old. He came to collect an ad, and Madam Nisa was not in the salon, so I gave it to him. He was a tall, 6-foot boy and seemed handsome. He came many times after that to collect ads or payments, and somehow, I had to deal with him each time he came. After visiting a few times, one day he rang me on the salon's landline number and told me that he liked me. I was a very reserved girl. In Pakistan, good girls are those who don't date or talk to any guys and marry wherever their parents want them to marry. I had this mindset ingrained in me, and I was not into talking to boys or dating. I was focused on my work and studies, which I continued privately. But when Nafees said that he liked me, I felt butterflies in my stomach. Although I told him at first that I didn't want to date, he still started calling on the salon number, and we started talking. One day, I agreed to go and see him. He picked me up on his bike after work, and we went to a nearby park. We had tea there. It was my first time going on a date with someone. I was nervous and shy. We didn't spend much time, and he dropped me off at the bus stop near my house.

I was never close enough to my mum that I could share my feelings with her, but somehow, I told her about Nafees. She didn't take it nicely and told me off. She was not interested in my marriage at that time because I was financially supporting my family, and my mum didn't want to lose the financial support I was providing by getting married. My two elder sisters married in their late teens. They were not working, and my mum felt burdened by them, so she arranged their marriages at a young age. Nafees didn't want a serious relationship or marriage at that time, and it was not an ideal time for me to get married because of my financial responsibilities. I also didn't want to get married at that time.

We met a few times, but our relationship didn't endure, and we broke up within a few weeks of seeing each other. Subsequently, Madam Nisa returned to America, and I moved to another salon, cutting off all contact with him. He was the only man to enter my life, and I never dated anyone else after him. I was still employed at the salon when, after a few years of our breakup, Nafees saw me at a bus stop one day. He was driving a car, but I didn't notice him and boarded the bus. He followed my bus and approached me when I disembarked. He greeted me with, "Hi, Seeme," (Seeme being my nickname) and asked how I was. I was shocked to see him after so long and couldn't converse properly. I behaved as though I didn't wish to engage with him. He didn't press further, simply returned to his car and drove away. However, I couldn't shake him from my mind once I returned home, despite my apparent disinterest.

A part of me yearned to reconnect with him. The temptation to talk to him again became overwhelming, and I couldn't resist. Although I didn't have his contact details, I knew the landline number of his office. A few days later, I called his office and asked to speak to Mr. Nafees. After a brief wait, he came on the line, and I apologised for my earlier behaviour, explaining that I was shocked and in a busy public place at the time. He accepted my apology and requested my phone number. I provided him with my recently acquired mobile number. We began sporadic phone conversations. Meanwhile, I had purchased my own salon and was working there. After a few months of phone conversations, he proposed meeting again. I agreed, and he picked me up near my salon one afternoon. We had lunch and went for a walk in the park. I had trained my younger sister in the salon business, and after a few years, she was capable of running the business independently. Despite any issues she had with me, she excelled in the hair salon business, and clients were satisfied with her work. When my mother noticed that my younger sister could manage the business, she began searching for a suitable match for me. When Nafees suggested meeting again, I informed him over the phone that my mother was actively seeking a marriage proposal for me and if he was genuinely interested, he should send his family to my house, as is customary in Pakistan. Nafees was hesitant to make any commitments, so I made it clear that I couldn't continue seeing him if he wasn't prepared for marriage. Consequently, we didn't meet for another year. I saved his mobile number in my phone under the name "Wrong Number." Whenever he called or messaged, I chose not to respond.

During that period, a woman accompanied by her two daughters visited me regarding a potential match for her son. On that day, I did not go to the salon. They sat in the living room, and my sister-in-law served them tea and snacks. I sat with them, and the woman asked me a few questions about my age and whether I could cook or manage household chores. After an hour, they departed. My mother decided not to disclose my employment or ownership of a salon, which I found strange. I insisted she should reveal everything about me, but my sister-in-law received a call from them the next day, stating they were not interested. I felt relieved. In Pakistan, girls working in salons, among other professions, are often perceived as 'not nice' girls, which I always found peculiar. Perhaps because working women have more exposure to life, they are more experienced, and it becomes challenging to control or manipulate them.

Despite the cultural and societal programming in my mind, I remained unconvinced by the concept of a fully arranged marriage, marrying someone I didn't even know. All my elder siblings got married that way, without even meeting or talking to their partners before marriage. However, I was not inclined towards a completely arranged marriage.

In the summer of 2007, Nafees called me again. I answered and explicitly told him that if he wasn't genuinely interested in me, he shouldn't call and waste our time. He assured me of his seriousness this time and mentioned me to his sisters, as he has five of them. I was sceptical and asked to speak to one of his sisters. He agreed to call me in the evening when he would be with one of them. In the evening, he called, and I spoke to his sister for a few minutes. She confirmed Nafees's feelings for me and his mention of me within the family. After this conversation, Nafees asked to meet, and we went for lunch. He expressed his desire to have his family visit mine to discuss our marriage. He appeared resolute and had decided he wanted to marry me.

I confided in my sister-in-law, Zara, about Nafees, and they agreed to meet him and his family. Nafees visited my house with his mother, brother, and brother's wife. This was a first in our family; a boy came to the girl's house for marriage arrangements. Surprisingly, my brothers and mother were accepting of this. Nafees's family was financially better off than us; he had a business, a good house, and a car. My family agreed to the wedding, and we had our Nikah ceremony (a paper marriage) in October 2007, with the actual marriage scheduled for December 2007. I was elated during my Nikah ceremony. I was still residing with my mother and was meant to move to Nafees's house after the main wedding ceremony.

After the Nikah, Nafees and I began seeing each other regularly, and we would talk on the phone for hours at night. Although my mother had initially agreed happily to my marriage with Nafees, she became extremely upset after the Nikah. Seeing me talking to Nafees and spending time with him upset her greatly. The three months between the Nikah and the wedding were a nightmare for me as I had to tolerate her behaviour. She experienced psychotic breakdowns again, constantly angry with me, unable to see my happiness, and doing everything in her power to bring me down. Some days, I couldn't bear to stay at home with her and sought refuge at my brother Adil's house for a few days. However, she even visited his house to reprimand me. Her focus was solely on me during that time, and I was under her scrutiny. She would swear, shout, and yell at me for hours, her behaviour extremely abnormal. I felt fearful in her presence, like a scared child, although she never physically attacked me. Despite my mother's issues, I continued talking to and seeing Nafees. I confided everything about my mother to him, but later I realised it was not a wise decision. It was the first time I had disclosed my mother's behavioural issues to someone outside our family.

During this period, my niece Aqsa had finished high school and was beginning college. She was not interested in becoming a beautician or hairdresser; instead, she aspired to focus on her studies and become a teacher. However, my mother insisted she join the salon after my marriage, wanting her to replace me and contribute financially, as I was leaving both the family home and the salon business. Initially, I supported Aqsa's decision to continue her studies, but as my mother's violence towards her escalated, I advised Aqsa to start attending the salon after her college classes to avoid further abuse from my mother. Reluctantly, Aqsa began going to the salon after her college hours.

My mother held a significant place in my life, and despite a nagging feeling that she might have mental health issues, I often believed she was right. However, the violence she displayed during my wedding preparations caused me to detach emotionally from her entirely. Our wedding date was set for the 28th of December 2007. On the 27th of December, we were engaged in pre-wedding rituals, including the henna ceremony. However, the atmosphere was far from celebratory; my mother's evident distress cast a pall over the proceedings, making it feel more like mourning than celebration. I lived in constant fear, apprehensive that my mother might do something dreadful at any moment.

My younger sister expressed happiness at the prospect of me leaving the salon after my marriage, as she would then manage the business independently and become its owner. However, it wasn't just my mother; the entire country seemed somber that day. On the 27th of December, the former female prime minister of Pakistan was assassinated in a targeted killing, sparking widespread protests and violence across major cities, including Lahore. All of Pakistan was shut down for the next few days, disrupting normal life and causing considerable inconvenience to many, including some of our relatives.

The venue we had booked for the wedding ceremony informed us that the function was cancelled due to the ongoing protests. In response, my brother contacted Nafees and requested him to come to my house with his immediate family so that we could proceed with the wedding there.

The 28th of December 2007, the day of my wedding, arrived amidst chaos and uncertainty. Few guests were present in our house, but my mother remained aloof from them, her emotions unclear. The atmosphere was devoid of any celebration or happiness. I got ready with a heavy heart, and even then, my mother attempted to conceal my gold jewellery, which I eventually found with the help of my sister. There was no warmth or joy in the air.

In the late afternoon, Nafees arrived with his family. My mother's reception of them was far from welcoming, and she didn't even bid them a kind greeting. As I prepared to leave my mother's house with Nafees, she didn't offer me a hug. Despite my attempts to embrace her, she pushed me away. As I departed, I couldn't shake the feeling of concern for my younger sister, brother, niece, and nephew, who would remain with my mother. Though they were teenagers, they were also victims of her behaviour. As I sat in the car with Nafees, navigating through blocked roads and protesters, I prayed for their safety. Thankfully, we reached our destination without incident.

The morning after my wedding, my sister-in-law Zara called me and mentioned they wanted to bring me home for a night, as is customary in Pakistani culture for newlywed girls to spend time at their parents' house. Nafees advised against staying at my mother's house, so I declined my sister-in-law's offer. My mother overheard the conversation and began shouting at me furiously over the phone. I ended the call abruptly. Later that afternoon, I had to visit my salon to collect a few belongings. Nafees accompanied me, parking his car outside the salon while I went inside. Upon entering, I was startled to find my mother waiting for me, her expression one of intense anger. I was so frightened upon seeing her that I couldn't even greet her. Hastily grabbing my things, I made my way back to the car. My mother followed me and, upon my entering the car, she grabbed the door and slapped me in front of Nafees, right there on the road. She refused to let go of the car door, and I felt a deep sense of sadness, embarrassment, and helplessness. Tears welled up in my eyes as I pleaded with her to let me go. Nafees stepped out of the car and confronted my mother, shouting and swearing at her. A crowd began to gather to witness the scene. Nafees's reaction escalated the situation further. I urged him to return to the car, and we drove away within minutes, but those few moments left a lasting impact on me. I sobbed like a child during the journey back home. After that incident, I avoided visiting my mother's house for six months.

When my youngest brother passed his 10th standard exam, I finally went to my mother's house with Nafees. She hugged me, and from then on, I started visiting her house, albeit not regularly.

Nafees and I lived on the top floor of the house, while his brother and his family resided on the ground floor. My mother-in-law had a room on the ground floor due to her health issues, which confined her to almost being bedridden. She was a kind and gentle lady. I took on the responsibility of caring for her, tending to her needs such as preparing breakfast, administering medications, and helping her with showers. Despite her health challenges, she never complained. Nafees's sisters visited frequently, and I made efforts to accommodate them and make them feel welcome.

My relationship with Nafees was characterised by my submissiveness and his authoritative demeanor. I endeavored to please him and obey his commands. In Pakistan, there were occasions when he slapped and physically assaulted me. Given my background in an abusive family, I considered this behaviour relatively normal, especially considering his household environment was not as tumultuous as my mother's house.

Nafees wanted me to work in his office and manage his business, so despite my reluctance and lack of understanding of the business operations, I commenced working at his office one month after our wedding.

Nafees disclosed to me after our marriage that he had been seeking to marry a wealthy woman to elevate his financial status or an educated woman who could efficiently manage his business. Failing to find such a match, he chose to marry me because of my education, hoping I would assume the role of running his business. There was a woman who previously worked in his office, but he terminated her employment upon my joining the office. Despite his expectations for me to manage his business, Nafees seldom engaged in any work at the office.

Shortly after our marriage, I began to recognise similarities in personality traits between Nafees and my mother, even remarking to him once that he exhibited habits reminiscent of my mother's.

Following our marriage, my mother's mistreatment of Aqsa escalated, despite Aqsa complying with my mother's wishes to work in the salon. Aqsa eventually reached out to me, expressing her distress and hopelessness, and informing me that she had left home and sought refuge at a friend's house. Despite my unwavering trust in Nafees at the time, I confided in him about Aqsa's situation and pleaded with him to assist her in her time of need. Nafees agreed, and I promptly went to rescue Aqsa.

Upon arriving at Aqsa's friend's house, I was startled to find my mother and sister-in-law already present, as they had also come to retrieve Aqsa. Aqsa remained hidden in another room, awaiting my arrival. Her friend informed my mother and sister-in-law that Aqsa was not present and aided Aqsa in escaping with me to my house. Aqsa subsequently began working in Nafees's office, but after a few weeks, she expressed a desire to leave my house and live with my second elder brother, her uncle, who had distanced himself from the family years ago. Surprised by Aqsa's decision but respecting her wishes, I allowed her to leave.

Later, I discovered that Nafees had been harassing Aqsa, prompting her departure to avoid disrupting my marriage. She resided with my brother for a few months before marrying someone she was interested in, ultimately choosing not to return to my mother's house despite my mother's attempts to reconcile.

Nafees's elder sister resided in the UK, and a few months into our marriage, we visited her there for a month. Although I enjoyed the experience, I never envisioned the possibility of living in the UK in the future.

After six months of our wedding, I became pregnant with my first child, and Raham was born in March 2009. Following Raham's birth, Nafees recognised that I struggled with his office work and business, so he opened a salon for me near his office. However, as a new mother, I found it challenging to focus on running the salon business, and unfortunately, it did not succeed. Due to my own childhood experiences and the hardships I endured because of my mother, I was determined to be a good mother to my children and shield them from the difficulties I faced growing up. I delved into parenting books, a practice uncommon in Pakistan at that time.

Tragedy struck when my mother-in-law was diagnosed with cancer and passed away three years into our marriage. Raham was two and a half years old when one of Nafees's brothers-in-law, a doctor, noticed that Raham's skin tone appeared slightly yellow, and he seemed shorter than expected for his age. Concerned, the doctor recommended a blood test, which revealed troubling results: Raham was diagnosed with thalassemia intermedia. The news hit me hard, plunging me into shock, sadness, and a period of depression for several weeks.

Witnessing the struggles of Nafees's friend, whose three children had thalassemia, was distressing. One of the children had tragically passed away at the age of ten, while the other two required frequent blood transfusions and faced significant challenges due to their illness. This experience compounded my fears for Raham's future. Although Raham did not have thalassemia major, the doctors cautioned us that thalassemia intermedia could lead to major health complications, including the need for blood transfusions at any point in his life. In Pakistan, thalassemia patients typically have a life expectancy of 10 to 12 years, and effective medical treatment options are limited.

Life became filled with worry, sadness, and overwhelming emotions for both me and Nafees. The doctors informed us that Raham might require a bone marrow transplant in the future, and if he had a healthy sibling, there was a higher likelihood of finding a suitable match. Several months later, I became pregnant with my second child. Undergoing fetal testing for thalassemia brought immense relief when we learned that the baby did not have the condition.

Chapter 3 - Breaking Free

Part I

Disassembling of myself

Nafees ended up in some kind of trouble, and Raham's illness made things worse to stay in Pakistan. We decided to move to the UK. It was not an easy decision, leaving your country where you were born, where you established your life, with its own culture and language, to venture into uncharted territory.

There are many people in Pakistan who want to move to other countries for a better life. Nafees and I had never been keen to move to another country. Nafees had his own business and a good social life. I had opened my salon business at home a few months before we decided to move to the UK, and it was going well. It was easy for me to work from home as a mom. I was living my life under the illusion that I was happy, like a sleepwalker unaware of what true happiness was. People say, ignorance is bliss, and that is exactly what it was like for me. How could I know what I was missing on when I had never experienced that before?

There were many big red flags I could see in Nafees, but I was in denial because the reality was too painful for me to acknowledge. I came to Nafees's house after burning all the bridges, so even the idea of going back to my mom's house was scary for me. My mom's house was nothing but a living hell for me. In the end, turning a blind eye to my husband's shortcomings seemed like the only option I had.

The world we live in is dominated by patriarchy, and in Pakistani society, male domination is at its peak. Nobody welcomes a newborn baby girl with the same warmth as they welcome a baby boy. Girls seem to be a burden for families. Some families even cry at the birth of a girl, including my own sister-in-law, who cried at the birth of her fourth daughter, even though she saw me financially supporting my family. I was not a burden for my family. I even bore all the expenses of my wedding and bought the dowry with my own money. But these few examples may not be enough to change the mindset of society and break the norms.

Growing up as a girl in Pakistan, you don't feel like your parents' house is truly yours. We were always told that one day we must leave the house. If we made any mistakes, we were told that one day we would go to our in-laws' house, so we were not supposed to make silly mistakes. We were taught to learn cooking, cleaning, and household chores at an early age because one day we would have to go to our in-laws' house.

When a girl gets divorced and returns to her parents' house, it's a huge burden for her parents, and she cannot go anywhere else as there is no safe environment for women to live alone. Even if a divorced woman works and supports her family, things are still hard for her.

I was emotionally too weak to face all of that. I was living my life in survival mode. The illusions I was living under were merely helping me to survive at that time. Although my lower self didn't want to come to the UK, my emotional self didn't realize that the universe had a better plan for my life ahead.

We sold all our possessions, gold jewellery, cars, furniture, and other household items. It was not easy for us. One day before our flight, my mom and my youngest sister came to see me, which I was not expecting from them. That was the last time I saw my mom until now as I write this.

I was crying as we left our house for the airport to catch our flight to the UK. One of Nafees's sisters and his brother came with us to say goodbye. Nafees's sister and I were crying when we bid each other farewell, and we went for check-in. I sat in the plane with a heavy heart. I was going to an unknown country, a new culture, and I didn't have any relatives or family members in the UK. Nafees's two sisters were already living in the UK. One sister had moved recently in those days. And then, after an 8-hour flight, my life completely changed. It wasn't just a change of country; Nafees also changed after that 8-hour flight. Or perhaps it was time to wake up from the dream and see his true face.

My second son, Aneeq, was born a few weeks after our arrival in the UK. We were living in a town in West Yorkshire. Life seemed so different here. Nafees was not allowed to work, so he stayed home most of the time. It felt like we were starting life from scratch. Nafees had a car, an office, and a bustling social life in Pakistan. He didn't take this change easily. He seemed upset with me most of the time and started behaving rudely. He had his two sisters who used to visit sometimes, but he talked to them regularly on the phone. Although I was busy with two kids, I felt lonely and isolated, with no one to talk to. Nafees started blaming me for everything. He wasn't good in English, so I had to do all the talking, which he didn't like.

Inferiority complex started creeping into Nafees's personality. He wouldn't like it if I talked to anyone, and would badmouth me or the other person whenever he would get the chance. I started going to college for a hairdressing course. This riled him up more, and he would reprimand me if I would dress up nicely for classes. Slowly, all his insecurities were coming to the surface, exposing what he truly was.

When we were dating, Nafees told me that he had a bachelor's degree in business. After coming to the UK, I found out that he couldn't even write Urdu properly. He was not educated, and he lied to me. How naïve I was to believe whatever he said about himself. Because I had a bachelor's degree and he was uneducated, this fact was what fueled his inferiority complex to extreme lengths.

Raham started having appointments with a haematologist for his thalassemia. The doctor here also told us that he might need a blood transfusion at some point in his life, but luckily, he never needed one, and thalassemia never affected his day-to-day life, except that he got tired quickly because of his low haemoglobin. Other than that, he was doing well.

I was totally dependent on Nafees in Pakistan, and the fact that I didn't want to go back to my mom's house under any circumstances made him feel secure. In the UK, he started feeling that I could leave him at any time and I could survive without him, and I didn't have to go back to my mom's house. Even though I never thought like that until he became extremely abusive. Which woman would like to leave her husband and father of her kids without any solid reason, just because she can survive without a man?

Because he was not working and not busy, I was his focus all the time. He criticised me and taunted me almost all the time. The more he criticised me, the more I tried to be nicer, so he wouldn't complain, but it never worked. Moreover, when he saw me trying to please him, he criticised and blamed me more, and one part of him seemed happy to see me trying to please him. I used to cook, clean, do all my household chores nicely and on time. I even put a glass of water near his bed every day so he could have his medicine. I was taking care of him like a kid, but he still tried his best to make me feel like the ugliest woman in the world. He also started talking negatively about my mom and about my family. What I told him about my mom's mental health issues, he used against me.

I was so naïve at that time. I started feeling bad about myself. He offered me my negative self-image on a plate and I bought it, in fact, welcomed it with both arms open wide. Maybe because, at least, there was something he could offer me? I started hating myself. I fell deep into the unforgiving cave of depression. There was no one I could talk to. It's very painful to believe that I am bad and I am not good enough. Even though I was going to college, because I was so depressed and lost at that time, I would hardly talk to anyone.

I was getting overwhelmed by shame, guilt, grief, and fear which are lower frequencies on the human emotional vibrational chart.

He became so controlling that I felt suffocated. He used to have the money, and he used to buy groceries. So many months would go by and I wouldn't even have one pound in my pocket, and only a few clothes in my wardrobe.

Then a few women in my neighbourhood found out that I am a hairdresser, and I can do threading. When I told Nafees about that, he became happy, and he set up a chair and mirror for me to work on. I was a little surprised by his reaction. When I did one small job and earned £10, I showed him the money, and he almost snatched it from me. I was not expecting that from him. I didn't say anything to him because I didn't want any conflict. I earned a few pounds after that, and he took away that money from me as well.

I always had high moral values. I was honest, loyal, faithful to him. I never lied to him, and I was never greedy. Witnessing such low-value behaviour from him was shocking and painful for me.

He started calling my high values my arrogance because I was not like him. He was feeling small in front of an honest, intellectual, high-value woman. To avoid his own pain, he was trying to change me. He wanted to take away my dignity, my values, so he could feel good. He wanted to feel like the superior one among us, so his ego could keep his inferiority complex at bay.

I was sacrificing myself, my peace, authenticity, but he couldn't take away my values. That was part of my being, and no matter how hard he was trying, he never succeeded.

I was tolerating his mental torture and verbal abuse, but when he started taking my money, I could not tolerate it anymore. I, somehow, accumulated the courage to tell him that I was not giving you money. That made him furious and he told me that I was not allowed to work anymore if I wasn't willing to hand over my hard-earned money. The irony in this still blows my mind away. Since I couldn't work anymore, I didn't have the money, which was proving to be the only light in a life enveloped by darkness. This was his way of claiming my being and proving to me once again, that he was in control of the unbreakable leashes of patriarchy that kept me "under control," even when we were residing in a much more liberal country. He didn't take away just my money, but also the little happiness I would gather by buying things that I liked such as nice clothes. He knew how much I loved dressing up.

He made me do things I didn't like and stopped me from doing things I enjoyed, and he used to enjoy doing that. He used to revel in seeing me in pain. Once, while eating a cupcake, he asked me to try it, and I declined, as I never liked cupcakes. He grabbed my mouth and forcefully stuffed the cake in, disregarding my refusal. At that time, I was emotionally weak; I never spoke up for myself. Saying no to him felt impossible. I did not have any sense of self; it was always about him—what he wanted, when he wanted it—I had to say yes. I was lost and confused.

In our first few months in the UK, he didn't hit me because he knew that here, the police could intervene, and he could go to jail for domestic violence. But then, one day, while he was yelling at me, I gathered the courage to reply to him. As soon as I said something to protect myself, he pushed me onto the bed and grabbed my neck with both hands, squeezing it tightly, threatening to kill me. After a few seconds, he released my neck and went downstairs. When I stood up from the bed, I blacked out for a few seconds. After that, something inside me started telling me that it's not just my fault; he is the troublemaker. Confusion grew bigger and bigger. Sometimes my mind told me that I was wrong, that I was the problem, and other times I started having negative thoughts about him. On a few occasions, I tried to stand up for myself and told him to stop abusing me. He became more furious after that and started blaming me more, which made me hate myself even more. Every time I tried to defend myself, he would use gaslighting, manipulation, and the blame game to make me feel more guilty. Burdened by guilt, I was the one who said sorry, hoping that if I apologised, things might get better.

He also used to say that he would harm the kids so he could see me in misery, agony, and pain, as he loved to see me suffer. And I started believing that he could do anything to see me in pain. My pain used to give him pleasure.

Even though I had been through many difficult times in my life, I never had suicidal thoughts before. This time, I started having suicidal thoughts. Hopelessness and helplessness infected my psyche. There were moments when I was about to ingest more than

12 different kinds of tablets to end my life, but thoughts of my kids stopped me. My little one was breastfeeding. Thinking about what would happen to him, how my kids would be traumatised, prevented me from committing suicide.

I was desperate to talk to someone. When there was no one to talk to, there was always one source I could turn to—God. I took refuge in my prayers. We had a small room in the house which I dedicated for my prayers. I started performing my prayers regularly. After my prayers, I would talk to God. In the beginning, when Nafees made me feel guilty, I prayed to God to make me a good wife and a good mom. After his physical abuse, I started complaining to God about him. I had faith that God was watching over me and listening to me. God was my only best friend at that time. Every time Nafees did something wrong to me, I would go to my prayer room and talk to God. Praying to God gave me peace in the midst of turmoil in my life. I remember one day, sitting on my prayer mat, I said to God that I put my case in your court, and I want justice. I don't know what to do, but you can guide me. I am too weak to defend myself, but you can defend and protect me.

The story of my childhood was repeating. Nafees was behaving like my mom, and even though I was an adult this time, I was not emotionally strong enough to stand up for myself. I showed up like a little scared child.

My depression was getting worse day by day. Then he started telling his family that I had depression and mental health issues because my mom and family had mental health issues. He started speaking against me to his sister. He convinced his sister that he was right, and that I was the problem.

When my depression got worse, to the point where it was hard for me to look after the kids and do house chores, he took me to the doctor and told them that I should stay because my mom has depression, so it's in our family history. I told the doctor that, and he prescribed antidepressant medicine and referred me for counselling therapy. He was not happy about me having counselling therapy.

In the beginning, for the first few months of our arrival, he used to behave rudely in front of his sister whenever they came over, so that he could show them that he had good control over me. In Pakistan, if a man looks after his wife and shows her love and affection, people call him a slave to his wife. In our culture, a man means you should have good control over your wife. Although it's not always the case, it happens most of the time. Nafees's behaviour was also stemming from his low self-esteem. He felt small in front of me, so to feel better, he started making me feel small in front of him and in front of his sister.

When things got worse between us, and I was at my lowest, he started treating me better in front of his sister. He started washing dishes when his sister visited. One of his sisters even said that they were very proud of Nafees because he was washing dishes for me, and they never expected that kind of good behaviour from him. I was quite confused and lost and couldn't tell her the reality I was living in. Even though I thought if I told her, she would never believe me because, in their eyes, their brother was right, no matter what. My both sisters-in-law who live in the UK were never mean to me. They were not negative like Nafees, but they were naive enough to believe his stories, whatever he told them about me.

Day by day his torture was breaking thick shield around me and I felt like disassembling myself to point that I was able to reach to my heart.

Part II

I Feel My Heart

One day, I was cooking in the kitchen; Nafees was doing something nearby when he asked me if I had added a certain ingredient to the dish I was cooking. I said no, and then suddenly he started slapping my face. It was so sudden that I became scared, like a child. When he noticed my fear, he started punching me. My elder son Raham was almost 4 years old at that time. Raham came into the kitchen, seeing me being beaten up by his dad, and he got scared. He started crying, holding his hands together and begging his dad not to hit me. When I saw Raham, I ran to the stairs to go upstairs. I didn't want Raham to witness all that. Nafees followed me, punching me on the stairs as well, and continued until I reached the bedroom. Raham remained downstairs. Nafees pushed me onto the bed and started punching the back of my neck. My body was shivering with fear. I felt like a scared, helpless child who couldn't protect herself. I had neck pain for many days after that.

That fear wasn't just because of him. I already had a little scared, wounded child in me that got triggered. After he was done, he went downstairs, and Raham came upstairs to see me. He was still crying. He asked me if I was okay. I hugged him and said, "I am okay, my dear. Don't worry."

My emotional pain grew bigger and bigger over time to the point where it was unbearable. One day, while cleaning the kitchen floor, I felt immense grief in my heart that I had never felt before, not even when my dad died. I broke down and started crying loudly. It felt like the grief one experiences when someone they love dies. It was the death of my illusions about our relationship, the death of the shield I had around my heart to avoid feeling my feelings, and the death of the old me so that my new, evolved self could be born. If I say I felt my heart for the first time, it wouldn't be wrong. There was so much pain and grief in my heart, buried and carried for many

31

years from my childhood, and of course, there was a new wound hurting my heart.

Raham was playing in the living room when he heard me crying. He went upstairs to tell his dad that mum is crying. Nafees came into the kitchen and started shouting at me, asking why I was crying. He said I was mad. He didn't have empathy for me, in fact, he didn't have empathy at all. I didn't keep quiet in front of Nafees that day. I said, "You crushed my heart with your continuous torture." I said it with so much pain, tears streaming down my cheeks, but I felt a little strong that day. When he noticed that strength in me, he took a knife and said he would kill himself. I knew he would never hurt himself, so I didn't pay much attention to his drama. Then he stopped; he was trying to make me feel guilty just because I was crying. I was not allowed to express my emotions. That day, I let myself process my grief. That pain and grief were too much to process in one day, but at least I started to acknowledge my emotions and began processing them.

As I started feeling my heart, I noticed my heart was bleeding, and there was so much pain in it. I had heard about the heart crying tears of blood; I was experiencing that. I started feeling that my heart was crying most days. I was hitting rock bottom, emotionally and financially.

My illusions about Nafees started shattering. I started to see glimpses of his real face. I could now see how he used to manipulate and gaslight me even in Pakistan, what he was trying to do with my niece Aqsa, why he shouted at my mum on the second day of our marriage so that I could never go back to my mum's house again. He used that situation to isolate me, to manipulate me as he wanted. I couldn't see his manipulations in Pakistan. My mind was foggy, but those clouds of fog started clearing up. I started seeing reality, and reality was very dark, painful, and intense. Our mind's job is to protect us from pain and to drive us towards pleasure, but in doing so, it takes us away from reality. If we run from pains, we never process them. Those pains stay in our system, affecting our being. That unprocessed pain also lowers our vibrations and disconnects us from our authentic selves.

32

He was giving me new traumas and pains, and old unprocessed traumas and pains were also surfacing. Yes, it was too much to handle, but when we show up as brave enough to go through that pain, we do get help from our source. No pain or any trauma is bigger than your soul. When we don't run away from our shadows, we face our fears and process our unprocessed emotions and pains, we heal ourselves. When we help ourselves, we also get help from other dimensions we can't even imagine.

I was taking antidepressants and going for therapy for a few weeks, but I didn't tell my therapist anything about Nafees at first because I didn't want him to get in trouble. Nafees had his doubts that I might tell my therapist about him, so he didn't want me to go to see the therapist. My therapist told me that if I didn't attend appointments for two weeks, they would discharge me because I had missed a few appointments. Nafees knew that. He didn't directly tell me not to go to see the therapist, but he left the house at my appointment time, so I couldn't go because of the kids. He used to look after the kids when I went for my appointment. He knew I couldn't go with the kids, so I missed that week's appointment. The following week, on my next appointment day, he was going to his sister's house for a few days. I had an appointment in the afternoon. He knew that if I missed that week's appointment, I would be discharged from the therapy service.

It was the 11th of June 2013. When I went to bed that night, I was broken to nothingness; I was shattered. I walked as if I were dragging my body. I had no energy. Seeing me as a broken, shattered, and weak woman was a pleasure for his ego. But one thing he didn't know was that behind this shattered and weak woman, a new strong, resilient, bold woman was being born.

When I woke up on the 12th of June 2013, I was a different woman. The clouds of confusion started clearing up, and the illusions were fading away. My mind was clear enough to see his manipulations, gaslighting, emotional, mental, physical, and sexual abuse. I didn't know where this sudden change and great courage came from that night. Were my prayers answered? After all, God does not come in human or physical form to rescue us. Sometimes he sends his blessings, angels, or even courage to us so we can help ourselves. Our prayers may not be answered the way we want things to happen. The universe works in its own way. God always listens to us, no matter what religious beliefs or faith we have. He may answer our prayers in his own way, with divine timing, or according to what is for our highest good. My prayers definitely got answered. Something from another dimension showered me with new energy of courage and bravery that night.

My body language was strong. The courage, the boldness, and confidence radiated from my being. It was the birth of the new me. Nafees was shocked to see me like that that day. He couldn't say any bad words to me. He was hesitant to talk to me. He couldn't stand in front of the new me, so after finishing his breakfast, he left the house. He came back with bags of food shopping. His body language turned into a pleasing mode. He showed me a pack of cherries and told me that he bought them for me because he thought that I liked cherries, which I didn't even know when I started liking cherries. I didn't say anything and showed him that I didn't care. After seeing me like that, he became fearful. I witnessed a fragile and scared man that day. Again, he couldn't stand it, and he left home without saying goodbye or anything to me. I saw him for the last time near the main door when he was saying goodbye to the kids. He went to one of his sister's houses in Manchester to stay for a few days.

I was completely done with him by that time. I decided to end this abusive relationship. Though it was not easy. We spent five and a half years together. We gave birth to two beautiful kids. I had good memories with him, even if there were more bad memories. I was anxiously attached to him. Leaving him was like tearing myself apart.

I also did not have any UK status. I was dependent on him. But I was at the point of my life where I didn't want to care about anything but to protect myself and my kids. I didn't know where my decision would take me. It was a leap of faith, or I was guided by grace.

I took my two kids with me for an appointment. Raham was 4 years old, and my other son Aneeq was 1 year old at that time. I told my therapist everything about him. When I was telling my therapist about him, I got so stressed that I started bleeding from my nose. My therapist encouraged me to call the police and gave me the police phone number. I came home with the kids, and I called the police. I told the police everything; they took me and the kids from that house, and we stayed in a hotel for two days. Nafees's sister called me on my phone when they found out about my police complaint, but I didn't answer.

I didn't want to talk to them or explain myself to them, and I also knew that they would never be able to understand me, so I changed my SIM card.

After living for two days in a hotel, we moved to a refugee centre. I was interviewed by the police about Nafees's domestic violence. Repeating all the details in the interview was more painful for me.

The kids and I stayed in the refugee centre for three days. It felt like staring life from scratch, I was sad, depressed, and anxious, but I was still trying my best to look after my kids very well. Raham was also upset and missing his dad.

I rang my brother and sister-in-law in Pakistan and told them what happened. They felt sorry for me. After staying in the refugee centre for three days, we moved to Leeds. I got refugee status to live in the UK because of domestic violence. The first few weeks were hard for me and for Raham. I was in a new city in a new country where I didn't know anyone. I felt chronic loneliness. I felt like I had been dropped into a new universe where there were so many people, but they were all strangers to me. I was experiencing all kinds of dense emotions: sadness, grief, loneliness, but that courage to fight never left me. One part of me knew that I did the right thing, and I never regretted leaving him.

Raham fell unwell and had a high temperature for a few days, maybe because of the trauma of separation from his dad. I was going through a lot myself, so I was not emotionally available for him as I should have been, even though I was trying hard to be a good mom at the same time.

After a few weeks, my youngest sister came to the UK after getting married. She came to London and visited me in Leeds for one week. Her husband was on a student visa, and they were struggling at that time. When she saw that I had UK status and was living in a house that was better than their accommodation, even though I was on benefits at that time, she didn't like it. Instead of giving me emotional support, she stood against me. She was giving me bad vibes, blaming me for everything that had happened. Even though I was not expecting too much from her because of my past experience with her, I still got heartbroken by her. I had hopes that she had changed, and that I would be embraced with warmth after going through something so tragic, but my own blood stood cold and heartless in front of me. I needed emotional support from her, but instead of offering some understanding, she tried to bring me down further. She reminded me of my mum: the same lack of empathy, the same negative dense energy, the same selfishness. It was so hard for me to tolerate her that I told her to call her husband and go back and out of my house.

When she left the house, she rang Nafees and one of his sister and talked against me with them. My sister-in-law Zara rang me from Pakistan and told me about that. It was heartbreaking for me what she did. My mind kept thinking, how could my own sister do this to me? Even though she never liked Nafees, when I broke up with him, she stood against me and took his side. Even though I was struggling emotionally, even after she saw me at my lowest, she was still jealous of me. My mind was thinking, Nafees and my mum were not enough in my life to show me enough negativity, and now there you go. My younger sister was hurled back at me, to further inject negativity in my life. However, I decided not to allow her negative energy to affect me.

I stopped talking to her after that and blocked her number. I heard from my family that she moved back to Pakistan with her husband because of their immigration issues. She tried so many times to contact me from Pakistan, but each time she reached out to me, I felt the same negative energy, to the point that I cut all ties with her and decided not to talk to her again in my life.

Chapter 4 – From Darkness to Light

It took me a few months to process what had just happened to me. In the beginning, I experienced anxiety attacks. Chronic loneliness, grief, and deep sadness seemed too much to handle at times. It was as if my hurt choked my very essence, carrying it into oblivion. I had never learned in my life how to embrace or process dense (negative) emotions. In the environment I grew up in, there was no space to express my emotions. I only learned how to bottle up or suppress my feelings. But something happened during my experience with Nafees in the UK. Something shifted in me, and as I realised that, this new tingling sensation in me scared me at first. Sudden changes, I feared the unknown, but fate is a stubborn little thing. It relishes on bringing you face to face with your worst demons, and as it chants, "fight!" Only then do we understand the weapons that dwell inside us to fight anything in the world, but for that, we have to look within ourselves for once – love ourselves for once.

Nafees caused me so much pain and triggered so many emotions in me that it came to the point where I couldn't suppress them anymore, so I started processing my emotions and feelings. I have witnessed people who run from the pain, they seek distractions. And I have seen women, when they come out of abusive relationships or when they have been victims in their childhood or with their partners, their mindset becomes a victim mentality. Being a victim or being in a victim mentality is a different thing. Yes, you can be a victim of someone's rage or abuse, but when you come out of that situation, you should not be stuck in a victim mentality because there is a great chance that your mind gets stuck in that victimhood, and it makes you feel pity for the rest of your life. This mentality follows you like a plagued shadow, reminding you of your pain, and in a surprising way, you latch onto it because it feels familiar. Even homely. Once that happens, it is very difficult to embrace that shift that took place in your mind and heart when you decided to leave your abusive relationship. The shadow comes in between. The thing is, that homely feeling is what caged you in your misery for the time that it did. And people, especially the ones who have been tainted with the ache caused by their very own, forget that just to feel a tinge of belonging as they step into the unchartered, daunting waters of loneliness.

In my case, Nafees's continual mental torture helped me to break the shield around me. I am not saying that any kind of abuse or torture can serve you. In most cases, traumas, emotional, and mental abuse can leave deep scars in your psyche that will take immense effort and deep healing to recover from. Every soul's journey is unique and has different kinds of traumas and unique ways of healing and dealing with those traumas. When your soul decides to awaken and evolve in this lifetime, the universe will send you the exact people and situations that you need at that time for your soul's evolution and according to the lessons you need to learn. In my case, I felt more alive after coming out from my rock bottom. But what I didn't know was healing is like peeling off layers upon layers like an onion, and I had just peeled the first layer.

I learned from my experience that a closed heart and a thick, energetic shield around you may protect you from pain, but it also prevents you from enjoying and feeling the beauty and wonders of life. As Osho, my favourite spiritual teacher, said, "when you avoid pain you avoid pleasure." Through my ordeals, I learned there is no happiness without misfortune. Only after you are struck with the heaviest of weights on your hard days, do you cherish the lightness of the good days.

When I left Nafees, I also left the victim of him behind. I was not afraid of my pain. I allowed myself fully to embrace my pains. I had been guided on how to handle and process my pain. When you embrace your pain and don't run from it, you realise it is not as big and impossible to handle as your mind was interpreting it. That happened to me. Within a few months, my loneliness, grief, and sadness started to diminish, to the point that I started feeling lighter and happier. As I faced my demons, looking them straight in the eyes, day after day as I healed, I learned I was stronger than them.

I bought my first smartphone and contacted my niece, Aqsa. We hadn't spoken to each other for a while. When she heard my story, she showed me compassion. I was happy to know that she is happily married and has two kids. She told me that she doesn't have any contact with my mum and with my family.

I didn't have much contact with my mum. Only sometimes when my sister-in-law, Zara, would ring me, she would give Mum the phone after talking to me. She would ask a thing or two, but most of our conversation was awkward silence. I would just exchange a few words with my mum and hang up the phone.

It was summertime when we moved to Leeds. The weather was nice and hot, so I used to take the kids to nearby parks. I found out about myself that I am not an introverted person. I love to interact with others, and I never struggle to make new friends. It helped me to settle in the new city. In the park, I met a woman named Sadia. She was living with her husband, and her kids were almost the same age as mine. She was from the same state (Punjab) of Pakistan where I am from. We became friends, and she invited me to her house. She was living near my house. Whenever I felt lonely, I used to go to her house with my kids. She always welcomed us, and her house felt like home. I made some other friends, and we used to invite each other's kids for birthdays and dinners.

Raham started school in September, and I was taking him to his follow-up appointments in the hospital for thalassemia every other month.

I started looking after myself. I started doing regular exercise and eating healthily. I stopped taking antidepressant medicine because I told my doctor I didn't need it. I was not depressed anymore.

I applied for a divorce, and I needed the address of Nafees to send him papers. I had never had any contact with him after leaving him, so I didn't know where he was living. I contacted the UK immigration office to find his address. They told me he had been deported to Pakistan. I sent the divorce papers to Pakistan.

Finding My Soul Sister

Raham started his primary school in September. Here in the UK, in primary schools, we pick up and drop off kids from classroom doors, and sometimes parents wait for a few minutes for the door to open. While waiting for Raham, I met a Pakistani woman named Sara. Her gentle eyes and warm smile made me feel at ease. We started talking more often, and soon, she introduced me to Rajni. Rajni's son was in the same year group as Raham but in a different class.

Sara was going to Pakistan for a visit, and while informing me, she told me that Rajni's story was kind of like my story, and she believed Rajni and I could be good friends. Rajni was born and brought up in India. We spoke the same language, Punjabi.

I invited Rajni to my house. We opened up in front of each other so easily. I poured out my story, and Rajni shared hers with equal candor. She told me that she was living with her in-laws and had one son and one daughter the same age as my kids.

In Rajni's presence, I felt comfort and a sense of home. Finally, I felt like I had met a member of my soul family. Growing up in my blood family, I often felt alienated. I knew I was different from the rest of my family, and here in the UK, I found my place.

Rajni and I developed an instant connection, and we became best friends in a few weeks. Rajni was going through a lot in her life, and she didn't have any friends. I was her first friend in the UK, even though she had been living here since 2000. When our common friend Sara came from Pakistan a few weeks later, she was delighted to see that Rajni and I had become close friends.

When Rajni came into my life, she embodied the qualities of loyalty, honesty, faithfulness, and sincerity like no one else I had ever met. After witnessing so much selfishness, heartbreak, and broken trust in people, I felt blessed to have her. Even though I had a few other friends when I met Rajni, the level of connection and comfort I experienced with her was unparalleled. My soul had been yearning for that connection, trust, and unconditional love, and with Rajni, I found it.

After emerging from rock bottom, Rajni's friendship was a gift from the universe. I truly believe that if the universe gives you trials (which are also good for your personal growth and evolution), it will also give you gifts. But mostly, people remember the trials and forget to count the blessings and gifts from the universe.

I want you to stop reading this book for a few minutes, close your eyes, relax, and pay attention to the gifts and blessings the universe has given you. For you, it may be your kids, partner, a friend, a house, good health, a good job, or, if you are very lucky, your parents.

In the books that I have read of Osho's, he says that if you have one person in your life with whom you can be yourself, share anything without fear of being judged, trust, be open and vulnerable, and feel safe and loved, then you don't need any psychotherapist. I truly believe that. Rajni is that person in my life.

Our personalities are so similar in many ways, and yet, we are different in many ways. Those differences we have also complement each other. If I am lacking something and not good in certain areas of life, I can always go to Rajni. Similarly, if she is not good at certain life skills and needs help, she would always come to me.

I have always had the courage and ability to make decisions. I started working at a young age, which made me an independent woman. Rajni came from a strong family system, raised by loving parents, but she was not raised to be an independent woman. Her parents live in India, and only her in-laws' family lives in the UK.

She needed that person with whom she could experience connection, motivation, encouragement, someone to listen to her and understand her. She told me I had all the qualities she really needed in a friend. She had all the qualities I needed, and I had all the qualities she needed. We melded into each other's life like a puzzle, and refused to let go, no matter what.

At the time we met, because of the challenges in her life, she was also going through depression. She really needed a good friend with whom she could talk, and feel heard and seen. When we became friends, she faced opposition from her in-laws. They didn't like her hanging out with me. They felt threaten by me because I was strong woman, and my emotional support will make her strong woman who will be difficult to control. She didn't care that much about their opinion. She was always welcome in my house, but I couldn't go to her house because of her in-laws.

I introduced Rajni to my friend Sadia, and then, Rajni, Sadia, and Sara became mutual friends.

One day, I received a letter from a solicitor that Nafees wanted to have contact with the kids from Pakistan. Reading that letter and thinking about him triggered all the memories about him. Everything came flushing back in my mind. I started crying after reading that letter. I didn't want to have any type of contact with him. At that time, I didn't even want to hear his name. I realised after reading that letter that my wounds were still fresh and unhealed.

I went to court for a hearing. He saw his brother-in-law and his nephew in court. They were dealing with his solicitor on Nafees's behalf.

I had a few hearings in court regarding the case, and Nafees didn't win. I was not in the state of mind to make the kids have contact with him. The kids were young, and to have contact with their dad, I needed to deal with Nafees, and I didn't want to have any contact with him. I was relieved when the case finished.

I used to take the kids to the local library, where I borrowed a book by the famous spiritual teacher Dr. Wayne Dyer. It was the first book I read about spirituality and personal growth. That's how I got into personal growth. In his book, he mentions the benefits of forgiveness. The idea of forgiveness just clicked with me as I read his wise words. It didn't take me much time to accept the idea of forgiveness as I was so captivated by the freedom it promised to offer. I was carrying a lot of anger and resentment towards Nafees, and it was hurting me. I wanted to forgive him, but not because of him. I wanted to forgive him for my own peace and liberty from the pain I was carrying because of his abuse. I didn't want to go back to him or forget what he had done. My forgiveness was for my sake, not for him.

I started forgiving him. I read in another book, imagine that person who hurt you standing near you, and you are telling him/her that you caused me so much pain and hurt me, I forgive you and set you free and set myself free. When you will be able to forgive that person, that depends on how deeply they have hurt you and according to the amount of pain you have been caused by that person. It might take one day, a few days, a few months, a few years, or even many years.

There was someone else who caused me so much pain and suffering from my childhood, and that was my mum. The idea of forgiving her didn't cross my mind at that time. There were two reasons for that.

The first reason was the pain she had caused me, it was too deep with its claws rooted into my very mind. I was not ready to process or access that pain.

The second reason was that in our society, we've been strongly told that whatever your mum does is right. Even when sometimes I used to complain about my mum to one of my brothers, he would always say she is mum, and she is right. Society has granted so many rights to parents, especially mothers, and there are not many discussions about children's rights.

I was always ambitious, a seeker of truth, and I was always curious to know more. But somehow, I didn't come across any books about personal growth, self-love, and forgiveness, or maybe it was not my time back then. Those personal growth books were a whole new world to me. It felt like my soul was craving that knowledge. One book led me to another, and I also started watching YouTube videos about personal growth. It was all about forgiveness, success, self-love, and happiness. That information was totally new and different from what I had been told all my life, and I was in awe. How come

I never came across such useful information about important life skills before?

It took me many months to forgive Nafees. I felt light and free after forgiving him. In the beginning of our separation, I used to tell everyone what he was doing to me because there was so much load on my chest, and I wanted to share. After forgiving him, I stopped talking about him unnecessarily.

My younger son started going to nursery. I was going to college for my hairdressing course. I also started working at a hair salon for just a few hours a day during Aneeq's nursery time. Life started feeling good.

Our friend Sara, who introduced me to Rajni, went back to Pakistan to settle down there. Rajni, Sadia, and I used to see each other every day at school, and we also used to visit each other's houses regularly.

Mine and Rajni's friendship was growing, and our connection was becoming deeper with time. Rajni's depression started getting better. She started working. Because she was living with in-laws, she wanted to have her own house where she could live only with her husband and kids. Finally, after many years, she and her husband got permission to buy a house. She was happy, and they started looking for a house. Rajni later told me that her life started getting better after I came into her life.

One day, I received a call from Nafees from Pakistan. By that time, I was okay to talk to him because I was on my healing journey, and I had forgiven him. I didn't tell him that I had forgiven him. I wanted to ask him if he had received the divorce papers, so I did speak to him. He said he received the divorce papers. He had signed them and sent them back. He told me that he got married a few months after going back to Pakistan. He said she is happy there and prefers to live in Pakistan. He didn't have any regrets about what happened between us. Even after all the agony that he had caused me, he still tried to make me feel bad. After talking to him, I felt low and depressed, like he had sent me bad energy over the phone. I blocked his number and decided not to talk to him again. I refused to let him affect my heart anymore. He sent the divorce papers after signing them to the court in the UK, and I received the divorce within two years of our separation.

I started enjoying my life with my two kids and with friends. I was not looking for a relationship or to get married again, but something big was waiting for me. Something that I had not imagined in my dreams.

Chapter 5 – Love, Lies, and Healing

Part I

Love

Slowly, I began to miss having family. Nafees came from a large family. Having come from a large family myself, now living alone with two very young children, I felt the absence keenly. Despite having friends, being the sole adult in the house made me feel as if I had no family at all, which contributed to my loneliness.

One of my friends mentioned that her husband knew a man who lived in Dewsbury. She described him as educated and a good man. She suggested that if I was okay with it, she could pass my number to him. He would then contact me, and we could see where things went. Without much thought or expectation, I agreed.

She informed me that his name was Haris and that he would call me at 6 in the evening. True to her word, at precisely 6 o'clock, Haris called. After a brief introduction, he explained that he was at work and had called because my friend had asked him to at 6. He inquired if he could call me later, to which I agreed, suggesting 9 o'clock when the children would be asleep, making it a more convenient time for me.

I appreciated his punctuality and was pleased when he called at 9 o'clock as promised. I shared with him details about my marriage and subsequent divorce. In turn, he revealed that he was born and raised in Pakistan but had come to the UK after marriage. However, his marriage lasted only a year before ending in divorce. He had no children and had been single for 14 years. Currently, he resided with one of his brothers, and most of his family lived in the UK.

We began talking on the phone daily, finding it very comfortable to converse, almost like talking to a friend. Our conversations were filled with laughter and enjoyment.

I informed Rajni and my friend Sadia about Haris. Shortly after, Rajni went to India for a month-long visit.

After conversing on the phone for a few days, Haris and I decided to meet. I invited him to dinner at my house. When I opened the door, I was greeted by a handsome, tall, and well-dressed man. He appeared to be educated, mentioning that he had obtained his law degree in Pakistan. Given my previous experience with an uneducated partner and how it had affected our relationship, I desired to marry someone educated.

The way Haris spoke, his mannerisms, his intellectual level, and his knowledge were sufficient evidence for me to confirm that he was an educated man. He introduced himself to the children politely. Raham was six, and Aneeq was around three years old at that time. We had dinner together with the kids. Dinner wasn't finished yet when Haris said, "I like you, and it's a yes from me." The way he expressed himself, every fibre of his being conveyed his fondness for me. He appeared happy and excited, as if he had finally found what he had been seeking for 14 years. I was a bit surprised, and I expressed uncertainty about remarrying and needing some time. He responded, "That's fine. Take as much time as you need."

After dinner, we visited my friend Sadia's house. Sadia also took a liking to Haris. Up to that point, I hadn't felt much about Haris. After leaving Sadia's house, we went for a long drive with the kids. During the drive, I felt a rush of energy within me, feeling attracted to Haris.

When he returned home, he called me and confessed that he really liked me and had become completely infatuated with me. The feeling was mutual. Having grown up watching Bollywood movies, where love stories often follow a certain narrative of overcoming difficulties, with the heroine and hero eventually coming together against all odds, I found myself embodying that Bollywood heroine.

I felt as though my prince charming had arrived after enduring numerous challenges, and everything would be alright.

We fell in love, which I later realised was more infatuation and trauma bonding than true love. The emotions were intense and irresistible. I accepted Haris's proposal, and we became engaged within a few weeks. My friend Sadia was delighted for me and hosted a small engagement ceremony at her house, attended by Haris's brothers, two sisters-in-law, and mother.

Meanwhile, Rajni was still in India. I missed her and sent her pictures of my engagement. She was surprised at how quickly it all happened but wished me luck.

I expressed to Haris that I loved living in Leeds, where I had friends, the kids were attending school, and I was enrolled in college. I stated that I didn't want to move to a new city. He assured me that I wouldn't need to relocate, and he would come to Leeds after we were married.

We had our Nikah, the religious marriage ceremony, in May 2015. My son Aneeq was three years old at the time, and he easily accepted Haris as his dad. Raham took some time to warm up to him.

Haris moved into my house after the wedding, and we began living together. Haris expressed a desire to have a child, as he didn't have any from his previous marriage.

A few weeks after the wedding, Haris mentioned that his brother and sister-in-law were unwilling to care for his mother, and he wanted her to live with us. I agreed, and his mother moved in with us. She was in her 80s and had numerous health issues. Haris had informed me about her physical health problems but had omitted to mention her mental health issues. I later discovered that her mental health problems were far more severe than just dementia.

With our house having only two bedrooms, I allocated our bedroom to Ama (Haris's mum) upon her arrival. Haris began sleeping in the living room, attending to Ama during the night when she needed help going to the toilet.

The more I accommodated Haris's wishes, the higher his expectations seemed to grow. A few weeks into our marriage, he started persuading me to move to Dewsbury. He argued that Ama was accustomed to Dewsbury and would be happier there.

Once the honeymoon phase and infatuation subsided, I began to feel that I had made a big mistake by marrying him. However, by then, it was too late, and I found myself pregnant with our third child. Even during the infatuation phase, there was a nagging feeling within me that something wasn't right, but I ignored my instincts. I didn't want to let go of the fairytale that I was so casually handed over by fate, only to realise it was, indeed, a nightmare waiting to happen.

I noticed discrepancies in Haris's words and actions. He claimed to be hardworking, but it soon became apparent that he wasn't. He ceased working after our marriage and spent most of his time at home without a proper job or career. He had never mentioned before marriage that his mother would live with us or that he wanted to reside in Dewsbury. When he suggested moving to Dewsbury, I expressed my reluctance, but my 'no' wasn't firm as I struggled to assert myself. He noticed this and persistently tried to persuade me until I reluctantly agreed. I informed him that I had enrolled in a hairdressing course at Leeds College, to which he suggested I commute by train as the classes were only once a week.

Haris didn't disclose to me that Ama had severe mental health issues. She suffered from depression, anxiety, paranoia, and hallucinations. She was never content and would constantly complain and mourn. Her energy felt dark and dense, bearing the same negativity and behavioural issues as my own mother.

Once, Haris and I were out with the kids for a few hours, so we left Ama at Rajni's house to keep her company. Upon Ama's return from Rajni's, she informed me that Rajni had spoken negatively about me. Ama claimed that Rajni had told her about me and how I orchestrated my ex-husband's deportation from the country. I was utterly shocked to hear this. I assured Ama that I had full trust in Rajni and she would never say such things. I made it clear that any attempt to turn me against my best friend would fail. Neither Ama nor I had ever discussed my ex-husband, so Haris must have disclosed my story to Ama at the start of our relationship. I was surprised that Ama remembered the details of my ex-husband's departure and was attempting to poison me against my trusted friend. I shared what Ama had said with Rajni, and she too was shocked, but our trust remained unshaken, despite Ama's dark and dense energy affecting me.

I hadn't realised that depression and negativity could be contagious. While caring for Ama around the clock, I began to absorb her emotions. I became so preoccupied with caring for Ama and Haris that I neglected my friendships, my self-care, and even reading books. Every day, I felt like I was losing a part of myself, descending further into darkness – the darkness of depression, anxiety, helplessness, and regret.

Yes, I started regretting marrying Haris. I regretted coming to the UK. I regretted becoming pregnant. I trusted Haris to understand my feelings, to protect me, and to make things easier for me, but my trust in him proved to be another illusion.

When I informed my friends that I was moving to Dewsbury, they were unhappy, especially Rajni. Although she couldn't explicitly tell me not to go, her sadness was palpable. Something inside me was resisting the move. My body and heart were reluctant, but my mind urged me to comply, to be the obedient girl who doesn't say no.

Rajni had moved out from her in-laws' house and into a new home not far from mine. She came to see me on the day I was moving. She was sorrowful, giving me a heartfelt hug and shedding tears. Her tears conveyed her need for me to remain in Leeds by her side, a need I failed to recognise at the time. Despite Dewsbury being less than an hour's drive from Leeds, neither Rajni nor I were driving at that time, making regular visits challenging.

Haris sat nearby, watching us with tears, yet I saw no sign of compassion on his face. He observed the unique and deep soul connection between Rajni and me, and I noticed he envied our friendship. When Rajni departed, he jokingly remarked that we looked like lesbians. I made it clear that I disliked his comment, reminding him that if that were the case, why would I have fallen in love with him and married him? It made me ponder the world we live in, where loving freely and experiencing the beauty of a deep soul connection is judged. Romantic relationships are often the most scrutinised, despite being the most challenging.

It had only been a few weeks since our marriage when I reluctantly moved to Dewsbury with Haris. He was good with my kids; I didn't witness any rudeness. He remained respectful towards me and the children. I felt obliged to see him interact well with my kids, but in return, I was sacrificing my own emotional well-being.

Part II

Prison with subtle punishment

Haris secured a house near one of his brother's residences, where he and his mother had lived before our marriage. The house had a spacious kitchen with a television and sofa. Haris insisted that Ama stay in the kitchen so that I could keep her company while cooking. With three adults and two kids in the house, I spent most of my time in the kitchen—cooking, cleaning, and washing dishes. Ama watched me incessantly, complaining and talking non-stop. The TV remained on, but her gaze remained fixed on me. I felt her intense animosity towards me. Her negative energy overwhelmed me, compounded by the hormonal changes of pregnancy, making me hypersensitive. I felt like a character in a stage show, suffocating under her scrutiny.

Ama was excessively attached to Haris, with him confiding that she was controlling and overprotective of him. Even in his forties, after our marriage, she disapproved of him spending time with friends outside the house. When he did, she pressured me to repeatedly call him to return home. Haris's brother's wife revealed that her husband had described Ama as always negative and controlling. She had a tough time dealing with Ama, which led to her depression.

Haris consistently sided with Ama, excusing her behaviour as dementia. Due to my mother's similar behaviour, I had a keen interest in understanding mental health issues. I had researched personality disorders, schizophrenia, and bipolar disorder. People with psychotic disorders like schizophrenia are more prone to developing dementia. In Pakistan, mental health issues are often disregarded, leading to individuals with severe mental health illnesses marrying and passing on their emotional wounds and trauma to the next generation. Ama's profound mental health issues and negative energy were draining.

My kindness towards others began to overshadow my own needs, and I did not realise I needed to show compassion to myself too. That house felt like nothing but a prison to me. I knew no one in the

52

city, and I disliked the town immensely. I felt out of place and lacked compatibility with Haris's brothers and sisters-in-law, despite their simplicity and kindness. I found myself tending to Ama like a nurse, administering her shower, medicine, and diabetic injections during my pregnancy, yet she never ceased her complaints and hostility.

My children were at an age where they needed their mother's attention. I was so preoccupied with pleasing Ama and Haris that I wasn't giving enough time and care to my own children. I ensured their physical needs were met and their safety was guaranteed, but emotionally, I wasn't fully present for them. Aneeq was adaptable and not very demanding, but Raham had a strong sense of self. He was a bright and intelligent child who sensed that something wasn't right, that Mum wasn't spending enough time with them. How could the children be happy if their mother wasn't?

Raham was the type of child who, if not given positive attention, would seek attention by annoying me. And he began to do just that. Due to my negative experiences with my own mother, I always aimed to be a good mother to my children, shielding them from the pain and traumas I had experienced growing up. Lacking many life skills at the time, I did my best according to my level of awareness then, allowing Raham to annoy me without fully understanding why he was acting out. All I wanted was to let him express his frustrations rather than suppress his feelings, so I made myself available to him, never attempting to silence him.

In that household, I was caring for everyone except myself. Everyone else was my priority except me. I was oblivious to the fact that there was not just me, but another soul within me, preparing to enter this world, and how my emotional turmoil could affect this new human being inside me. Ironically, the father of this child seemed uninterested in providing a safe and happy environment for me.

I became dependent on Haris for my happiness, peace, and emotional well-being. The accumulation of unresolved emotions, sudden changes in my environment and life that were not in alignment with my true self, and being engulfed by negative energy, along with hormonal changes in pregnancy, led to panic attacks.

I began experiencing severe panic attacks. I had suffered from anxiety attacks in the past when I left Nafees, but these panic attacks were different and much more challenging to handle. During a panic attack, I felt as though I was dying, struggling to breathe and overcome by a sense of suffocation. My body was trying to communicate with me, but I wasn't listening. Our bodies have their own intelligence systems, and when something is wrong, they find ways to alert us, but do we heed their warnings?

When I had my first panic attack, I wasn't even aware that I was experiencing one. I was busy working in the kitchen and didn't stop to acknowledge it. I didn't allow myself to recognise the panic attack, although it was unavoidable. I didn't permit my body to feel what it needed to feel at that time, nor did I listen to what my body was trying to communicate to me. When Haris arrived home and saw me, he inquired why I was in a bad mood. I couldn't answer him because I didn't even understand what was happening to me. When he noticed my lack of response, he became displeased. Once I recovered from the panic attack, I explained to him that I didn't know what had happened, but it had been a terrible experience. I expected him, as an educated and sensible man, to listen and understand, but I was surprised to see that he became agitated.

He didn't shout or yell at me, but his facial expressions indicated that he didn't believe me. He conveyed the message that whatever I was feeling didn't matter, or perhaps I was simply acting.

I came to realise through Haris's discussions about Ama and from living with Ama that she always sought attention by feigning illness. He informed me that Ama would sometimes faint suddenly and then recover within minutes.

Growing up in such an environment, Haris developed the belief that all women pretend to be sick to garner attention. He never showed concern if I fell ill or inquired about how I was feeling. Whenever I mentioned feeling unwell, whether with a fever, headache, flu, or even panic attacks, he paid no attention, as if I were lying to him. I found this behaviour very perplexing because I am not someone who enjoys lying, and I would admit if I were genuinely unwell. For minor ailments, I preferred not to inconvenience anyone. He failed to understand who I truly am. He didn't see me for myself; rather, he viewed me through the lens of his own preconceptions, shaped by societal norms and influenced by his mother.

Because Haris was good with my kids and always respectful towards them, I chose not to acknowledge the negative aspects of his personality. I felt like I had no other choice but to keep swallowing bitter pills, hoping, praying, that someday I might taste something sweet.

I used to speak to Rajni and my friend Sadia on the phone, but with time, our contact dwindled. I missed them terribly, but with everything that I was dealing with, this ache had taken a backseat, only resurfacing from time to time.

One day, while I was working in the kitchen, Ama continued to stare at me. The hostility in her eyes infected my heart, and her constant complaints tortured my mind. Overwhelmed by negativity and unsure how to protect myself, I couldn't bear it any longer and began to cry. Tears of pain and helplessness streamed uncontrollably down my cheeks. I felt claustrophobic – like I had nowhere to go where I could be alone, myself, and miserable without a set of eyes following my every move.

Haris was in the living room with the kids. Upon hearing me cry, he entered the kitchen and asked what had happened. Instead of showing compassion, I perceived frustration on his face. Once again, he showed no concern for my well-being and indicated that I shouldn't display my emotions.

At this point, I had enough, and I explained to him that as she is an elderly lady, I am pregnant and require space. I couldn't divide 24 hours into being a wife, a mother to two children, a pregnant woman, and a nursing maid to his mother anymore. Surprisingly, he agreed to my pleas and made arrangements with his brothers. Ama would spend two weeks at their house and two weeks with us.

After a while, he suggested that I open a salon so I could work while he stayed home to look after the kids. He began searching for a shop, and we visited one together. However, being pregnant and struggling emotionally, I wasn't enthusiastic about starting a business in that state of mind.

In March 2016, my youngest son, Talal, was born. Seeing his adorable face, I felt ashamed for ever regretting my pregnancy. Talal is a beautiful, evolved soul who brought blessings, love, and joy into my life. Rajni visited to see Talal and brought gifts for him.

Over a year had passed since I moved to Dewsbury, and I still didn't enjoy living there. The town simply wasn't for me. One day, I expressed to Haris that I wanted to move back to Leeds. He promised that if I didn't like living there after a certain period, we could return to Leeds. So, I reminded him of his promise. However, he became angry and spoke rudely to me for the first time. He claimed that I had done "nothing for him" and accused me of always being agitated.

Although we didn't engage in major arguments, he abruptly ended the conversation. Following this exchange, I had an intuitive sense that he had some psychological issues, and his words, "you did nothing for me," remained ingrained in my mind. I had been sacrificing my happiness, peace, and everything I could offer, hoping that one day he would appreciate and validate my efforts. Yet, here he was, claiming I had done nothing for him.

Part III

Spiritual Awakening

For the next few days, I pondered over what he had said to me, and then something within me stirred. It felt as though I had been in a deep slumber all my life. The illusions surrounding Haris began to dissipate, and my mind gained clarity. I started to see through his manipulations, having realisations and insights into his actions.

When you experience awakening and your soul begins to communicate with you, these insights become crystal clear, leaving no room for doubt.

I realised that he desired to isolate me so that he could manipulate and control me as he pleased. He was envious of my bond with Rajni and sought to sever our friendship. However, he understood that he couldn't simply instruct me to end it. Instead, he removed me from her and my other friends, knowing that my social circle was a source of strength. He knew that my friends could offer me perspective, making it harder for him to exert control over me.

Initially, I wondered why he was jealous of Rajni and our friendship, considering he was my husband and should have been my priority after my children. But then it dawned on me why he felt threatened. Rajni and I shared a profound soul connection, a rarity in this world. Our connection was meant to facilitate mutual healing and spiritual growth in this lifetime.

In contrast, my connection with Haris was superficial, more of a meeting of minds rather than souls. One mind sought to dominate, while the other was easily influenced.

We all yearn for deep soul connections with others, but many lack such connections because they are disconnected from their own souls and the source of their being. Most people are driven by their egos, which hinder genuine connections with others, leaving them feeling empty inside.

I also realised that he was using Ama to keep me confined at home. He wanted me to be preoccupied with Ama so that I would forget

57

about myself and my friends. He preferred not to directly inflict mental anguish upon me, so he manipulated the situation through Ama. This way, he could torment me mentally while appearing to be a dutiful son in the eyes of others. If I dared to complain about Ama, he could easily make me feel guilty by invoking her age and supposed rights. He had employed similar tactics with his brother's wife, and after marrying me, he brought Ama into our home to serve as a tool against me.

Ama's mental health issues could have been handled better because she was an elderly lady, but he was the one who was making things difficult for me. Now it was time to take charge of my life and make things easier for myself.

When I came to Leeds for college, I visited Rajni and Sadia. When I confided in them about Haris and what he was doing, they revealed that they were already aware that he was trying to separate me from my friends to isolate me. I was surprised to learn this. They explained that they hadn't told me earlier because they believed I wouldn't have believed them at the time, and they didn't want to jeopardise our friendship.

I visited a property dealer's office and found a house for rent in Leeds near my friends' house.

That night, when I returned to Dewsbury, I made the decision to confront Haris. The strong, resilient woman within me awakened, and I resolved that I would never lose myself again for someone else.

This time, I had the courage to speak my truth without fear. When the children went to bed, I confronted Haris about everything he was doing. I laid bare his manipulations. I was so confident, bold, and determined that he couldn't say much in response. He was stunned to see me so strong, and signs of defeat appeared on his face. He felt defeated because his manipulations hadn't worked. He hadn't tried to win my heart; he had attempted to control my mind with his manipulations.

In the end, I informed him that I was going to Leeds. I had seen a house, and if he wanted to join me, he was welcome. If not, I didn't care. After saying that, I went upstairs to bed.

In the following days, I moved back to Leeds in January 2017. Haris came with us and assisted with the necessary arrangements. I prayed to God for the children's school admission in the nearby school they had left a year and a half ago, and they were admitted to the same school within two weeks. I began seeing Rajni daily at the school.

Leaving the prison that Haris had created for me made me ponder whether it was a prison of my own mind. My mind wasn't truly mine; it had been programmed, hijacked, and polluted by others. Our parents, society, and the environment we grew up in conditioned us to fit their agenda. They instilled in us the belief, especially in women, that being a "good girl" means not saying no. A "good girl" sacrifices her happiness, joy, peace, and emotional well-being for others. She lives her life for others, prioritising everyone else above herself. She doesn't even own her own mind and body—her mind is controlled by others, and she is made to feel ashamed of her body.

I resolved to take charge of my mind and never allow it to be controlled by others. I decided to live my life according to my own rules.

My true quest for truth began. I realised society had led me to believe in lies that did not serve me. I needed to uncover the truth. I was willing to pay any price to discover the truth of "who I am".

I began looking after myself, adopting healthier eating habits and exercising regularly. I focused on personal growth by reading books and watching videos about healing and mindset.

I established a morning routine, waking up at 5 a.m., exercising, and reading before the children woke up. I still maintain this morning routine with some modifications.

I started reconnecting with my friends regularly, and life began to feel better.

I encouraged Haris to find work, and he started working regularly. Ama would come to stay in our house for two weeks, and while I continued to care for her, I prioritised my emotional well-being. If I felt overwhelmed, I created space for myself. She was no longer in the kitchen with me; instead, she stayed in the living room while I retreated to my bedroom to read if I needed space and rest. My friends began visiting me, and I started visiting their homes regularly.

I discovered the Six Phase Meditation by Vishen Lakhiani on YouTube and began practising it. One part of the meditation involved forgiveness, where you imagine the person who hurt you and forgive them to find peace and healing. Reflecting on my painful experiences in Dewsbury and Haris's manipulations, I decided to forgive him, as he seemed to be behaving better in Leeds. I visualised him in my meditation and forgave him.

After settling in Leeds, Haris behaved well for the first few months. I didn't realise at the time that a person with a negative mindset can never give you a positive life, and that negativity can manifest in various ways. Naïvely, I told Haris I had forgiven him, to which he laughed and dismissed, saying he had done nothing to warrant forgiveness.

I wanted to forgive everyone who had hurt me because I wanted to free myself from suffering and pain. When we don't forgive, we carry that pain, anger, frustration, and grudges throughout our lives. Yes, sometimes forgiveness is difficult. In my case, when I started to forgive my mother, my inner child wasn't ready, so instead of forcing forgiveness, I focused on healing the emotional and psychological damage my mother had caused.

When Raham turned 8 years old, he still didn't know he had thalassemia. One day, he asked me why his little brother Aneeq didn't need to go to the hospital for blood tests like he did. I explained to him that he had a condition, but it wasn't severe. Upon learning he had thalassemia, a lifelong illness, he became upset and started complaining. I reassured him that he wasn't an ill child and could achieve anything in life. Despite his condition, he could still pursue his dreams. Initially, he stopped doing activities he enjoyed, blaming thalassemia. I continued to encourage him, reminding him of his abilities. Eventually, he stopped complaining and resumed behaving like a healthy child. Although there was a possibility of him needing a blood transfusion around age ten, he never required one. The doctor praised me for taking good care of him, stating that his well-being was a credit to my efforts and that thalassemia hadn't significantly impacted his life.

Haris's behaviour towards me and the children began to change. He appeared unhappy, frustrated, and indifferent. I never felt seen, heard, or valued in this relationship, and now I felt even more unloved. He wasn't pleased that I was asserting my independence and living life on my terms without his control. As I became a stronger woman, he lacked the courage to verbally abuse me, so he resorted to expressing his frustration in subtle ways.

The more I improved myself through self-work, the further apart we grew. As the distance between us widened, he also distanced himself from my children. In Dewsbury, he had been good with them because he was in control there. His manipulation tactics were effective, and he took pleasure in seeing me emotionally affected by his mother.

The atmosphere in our home became tense. No one was happy anymore, including the children. I decided to have a difficult conversation with Haris. When the children were asleep and he was watching TV, I approached him. However, he seemed disinterested in talking. After a few words, he abruptly suggested we separate. It caught me off guard, and I didn't say much as he didn't seem interested in resolving our issues. I calmly accepted his decision, saying he could go if he wanted, and then I went upstairs.

Something inside me shattered. I didn't want to end the relationship; I wanted it to work. Although I hadn't considered separation before, I didn't resist his suggestion. I began to contemplate and reluctantly accept the idea of separating from him, even though it was painful.

The next morning, tears in my eyes, I took the children to school. Rajni met me there, I told her about Haris leaving.

Upon returning home from school, Haris was packing Ama's clothes. I helped him pack, and he left with her.

That evening, he returned alone as if nothing had happened. I was still in shock and processing my emotions, so I didn't show any happiness at his return. He apologised to me, claiming he didn't want to separate.

His apology didn't appease me; I knew he didn't mean it. He informed me that Ama would not return to stay with us. I had a realisation of his intentions. He understood that despite his manipulations, I hadn't considered leaving him. He assumed that because it was my second marriage, I would avoid divorce and beg him to stay if he mentioned separation. He planned to exploit this weakness to keep me under his control indefinitely. Removing Ama from our home was part of this scheme; he couldn't use her to torment me or confine me to the house any longer. Although I continued to care for Ama, I refused to let her affect me, and he resented that. He wanted me to live in pain and misery, as some people derive satisfaction from seeing others suffer.

I still wanted my marriage to work, but things were deteriorating over time. The distance between us was growing, and I began to feel stressed. However, this time, I didn't stop working on myself. I continued with my meditation, exercise, and reading.

Something within me was changing. My consciousness was expanding, and my perspective on things was shifting. I gained more clarity in my perception. I began to work on my self-esteem and started affirming to myself, "I am enough in my being." I plastered this affirmation everywhere in my house, even in the toilet. I set it as wallpaper on my phone.

Despite my efforts, things didn't improve between Haris and me. One day, I told him that I needed space and suggested separation to see if things would improve with some distance. He went to Dewsbury to live and began visiting on weekends. Because I was working on myself and changing, I believed that people could change. I started attempting to change him, sending him videos about personal growth. He started behaving nicely, and I thought he was genuinely improving. I allowed him to come back home, thinking my efforts were working. So, after a few weeks, I suggested he move back in with us.

He returned in November 2017, and his temporary sweetness soon turned bitter. He didn't want to lose me, yet he couldn't find happiness with me either. Perhaps because he was unhappy inside, and we can only give what we have. Wounded people tend to inflict wounds on others, and although I wasn't willing to accept any more wounds and trauma, I was still affected by his negative energy. My relationship with Haris was dragging me into darkness, but I persisted in working on myself, seeking answers and light amidst the darkness.

Haris offered to look after the kids so that I could pursue my dream of opening a salon business. I agreed, and I began searching for a suitable shop. I found one with a residential flat upstairs. Haris, being knowledgeable about building work, started renovating the shop for me.

One night, as I lay in bed, I felt intensely lonely, despite Haris sleeping beside me. I questioned the nature of our relationship and whether I deserved to be in such a situation. Feeling the need to talk to someone, but not wanting to disturb anyone in the middle of the night, I suddenly felt the presence of my dad's spirit in the room. It was a profound moment; I felt emotional, as if reuniting with my dad after a long time. His voiceless reassurance comforted me, telling me I wasn't alone and that everything would be okay one day. Though I initially wondered if I was imagining it, years later, a psychic medium confirmed that my dad's spirit was always watching over me from the spirit realm. Perhaps it wasn't just my imagination; perhaps my dad's spirit truly visited me that lonely night to offer solace.

I decided to do an inner child meditation to heal my inner child. In this meditation, I closed my eyes, and my adult self revisited the house where the abuse occurred to meet my five-year-old self. I asked her how she felt and allowed her to express all her emotions and feelings with compassion and without judgment.

A flood of emotions and tears overwhelmed me during this visualisation. The little girl inside me expressed feelings of being unloved, uncared for, scared, sad, and worthless. I allowed her to express herself fully. When she finished, I brought her back to my present house and reassured her that she was enough, worthy of love, and safe. I promised to take care of her and encouraged her to relax and be playful while I, as her adult self, took charge of my life.

I don't know for how long I sat in that meditation. I felt a shift within me after doing it. I repeated the meditation a few times over the next few months until my inner child felt better and I found myself not crying during the practice.

My healing and personal growth were causing a greater mismatch between me and Haris. When he couldn't control me despite his attempts, he started behaving poorly towards my kids. He was okay with his own son, Talal, but I noticed he wasn't treating my other two sons the same way. He didn't display his bad behaviour in front of me, knowing I was a protective mother. I attended college for my media makeup course once a week, leaving him to look after the kids. Something wasn't right during those days.

Raham and Aneeq were emotionally disturbed, and I noticed signs of trouble. Despite my efforts to be a good mother, chaos reigned in our house. My relationship with Haris was crumbling. Raham, just 8 and then 9 during this period, had a strong personality and wasn't fearful. I sensed that Haris disliked his boldness and began to show disdain towards him. Raham, in turn, displayed defiance, sparking a silent competition between an 8-year-old and a 46-year-old. Haris couldn't verbally abuse him in my presence, knowing my stance on emotional well-being, yet tension lingered between them. I tried to support Raham emotionally, but nothing seemed to work, and he began acting out.

My efforts to create a haven for my children turned into a nightmare of chaos, tension, stress, and instability.

As I focused on my children's well-being, I distanced myself from Haris. Seeing this, he tried to offer what he could to please me, focusing on renovating my shop. I realised he didn't want to lose me; he wanted our relationship to succeed, but neither of us possessed the necessary relationship skills. He had grown up in an extremely dysfunctional and physically abusive family, lacking love and compassion.

The renovation of my shop was nearly complete when one day, while watching a makeup tutorial on YouTube, I stumbled upon a video about the signs of narcissism in February 2018. Another video followed about codependency, and I recognised all the signs within myself. I discovered that I was codependent, and codependent people often attract narcissistic partners, especially in romantic relationships.

I observed similar traits of codependency in Rajni. Realising this, I shared my findings with her, and she agreed she exhibited the signs.

As the situation in my house worsened, I opened my salon in February 2018. While it was a dream come true, I felt stressed and overwhelmed on the opening day.

During one evening in the living room, Raham said something to Haris. Though he remained silent, his eyes and body language conveyed his feelings. I witnessed the hatred in his eyes towards Raham and its impact on him, a nine-year-old's heart crushed and his body restless. Although there was no physical violence, an intense, non-verbal emotional abuse permeated the room.

Wanting the relationship to work because there was no physical abuse, as I had experienced in my past, I failed to recognise the emotional abuse occurring. Emotional abuse can be as painful and damaging, if not more so, than physical abuse. It's subtle and not easily visible, requiring clarity of mind and awareness. Unfortunately, I lacked such awareness about emotional abuse and its detrimental effects on mental health. There are various forms of emotional abuse, including manipulation, gaslighting, showing hatred, and controlling behaviour, all of which I wish I had understood earlier.

I had a conversation with Raham, explaining to him that if someone hates you, it's not about you; it's about them. They hate themselves and don't know how to love. I reassured him that he is lovable, that I love him, and I will protect him.

Making the decision to end that relationship wasn't easy for me. I had recently opened a salon because Haris was supposed to help me with the kids and the house so I could run my business. With three young children, including a two-year-old, and our impending move to the flat above my salon, I needed his help with the logistics. I knew things would be difficult for me after leaving him at this moment, but continuing to live with him in that situation had become intolerable. I was prepared to face any difficulty that life threw at me after letting him go from our lives.

The next morning, after dropping Raham and Aneeq at school and Talal at nursery, I went to my salon and called Rajni. I informed her that I was ending things with Haris and needed her emotional support as it wasn't an easy decision for me.

She was at work but took time off to come to my salon. Meanwhile, Haris was at home, so I called him and asked him to come to the salon. When he arrived, I told him I was ending the relationship and that he needed to leave. Although he seemed shocked and upset, he didn't say anything rude. I informed him that he could pick up Talal every weekend, and he could spend time with him then. I also instructed him not to inform any of my friends; if anyone needed to know, I would tell them myself. He accepted my decision, stating that he didn't want to end the relationship, but he respected my choice. He assured me that his door would always be open for me before leaving.

As he departed, I felt as though my heart had been crushed. I hugged Rajni tightly and began to cry. It was the first time in my life that I had someone's shoulder to cry on who could understand and show compassion towards me. I felt comfort and maternal love from Rajni—a type of love I had never experienced before in my life, now being offered unexpectedly by the universe. I cried with intense pain for several minutes, and she continued to comfort me until I began to feel better.

Chapter 6 – Price of Independence

When Haris left the salon after gathering his belongings from home, he headed to my friend Sadia's house. Sadia and her husband took his side, which didn't surprise me in the least. I had cautioned Haris against confiding in any of my friends because I was asserting myself as a strong woman. Sadia's husband harboured disapproval towards me; in his view, I represented a negative influence on his wife, potentially instilling in her a strength that defied control.

The following day, Sadia called me to express her disagreement. She reminded me of my second marriage and fretted over what people might say. I brushed off her concerns, asserting my indifference to public opinion. She then insisted that it was a woman's duty to sustain a marriage by turning a blind eye, making compromises, and tolerating a man's misconduct. I countered, stating firmly that I refused to conform to such expectations. I had compromised in the past to no avail and vowed not to repeat the mistake. Despite her persistence in convincing me otherwise, I maintained my stance.

I acknowledged the possibility of my own faults, pondering whether I attracted the wrong kind of men or invested too much without reciprocation. Yet, I reminded Sadia that regardless of my faults, as a friend, she should provide me with emotional support during my challenging times. Once I regained composure, she could offer her insights on where I may have erred. That, I insisted, was what good friends did.

Our conversation lasted about an hour, during which she persisted in trying to undermine me, despite my heartache. However, I stood my ground, defending myself with unwavering conviction. My tone and demeanour exuded strength, a quality she seemed uncomfortable with.

She then criticised my decision to open a salon business, deeming it misguided. In response, I pointed out the hypocrisy in her judgment, highlighting that just as I refrained from judging her role as a housewife, she had no right to criticise my career choice. We were different individuals, and I had been a working woman throughout my life.

When she realised her attempts to discredit me were futile, she resorted to a different tactic, remarking on my silence towards my children. By this, she meant that I didn't scold or berate them, especially in front of others. I firmly believed in respecting my children and refraining from publicly admonishing them. In contrast, she had a habit of shouting at her own children, leading her to judge my approach as neglectful of my kids' self-respect and emotional well-being.

I retorted that just as I refrained from judging her parenting style, she had no authority to criticise mine. I had my own methods of instilling values in my children, which didn't involve shouting or humiliation.

Then I reminded her that I am going through the pain of a breakup, and yet you're telling me that everything I'm doing is wrong, and you're offering support to my ex. What kind of friendship is this?" I hung up the phone.

I knew Sadia didn't appreciate my inner growth. She disliked me becoming a strong woman. I noticed she wasn't happy at my salon opening ceremony. But I had no idea she would let me down in my time of need and support Haris.

I'd heard that weak men don't like strong women, but it was disheartening to realise that a woman wouldn't like another woman to be strong. That was heartbreaking for me.

I felt betrayed and deeply hurt by her, so I decided to end my friendship with her and block her number.

In the next few days, I moved to a flat upstairs from my salon. I asked Rajni's husband and one of my other friends' husbands to help with the move.

I started researching about codependency and narcissism as if my life depended on it. The more I delved into codependency, the more

I understood myself. And the more I understood myself, the more my self-image shattered before my eyes.

I realised that my self-image, my perception of myself, my identity, were all false and stemmed from codependency. All my life, I'd held onto an image of being a good girl, only to discover it was just a façade of goodness. It was painful to accept that I am codependent and emotionally and psychologically unhealthy. I didn't resist accepting that I am codependent. Not only did I accept that I am codependent, but I also accepted that I am responsible for my misery and suffering. It was the bitterest pill to swallow, but at least there was hope that if I am responsible, I can change my reality by changing myself. I tried to change Haris, and it didn't work. I came to the realisation that I can't change others if they don't want to change themselves, but myself is my responsibility, and by changing myself, I can change my life, and I deserve a better life.

In the next few months, I endured the pain of my second marriage breakup, the betrayal from my friend, and the shattering of my self-identity. I kept going in my life with pain because I was a mum of three kids and the owner of a new business. My kids and my business demanded my time and attention while I was in emotional turmoil and pain. I used to drop the kids off at school and nursery, then open my salon and work until evening. A few times when the pain felt too much to bear, I went upstairs in my house from the salon to cry, and when I felt better, I returned to the salon.

Knowing about narcissism was shocking and painful at the beginning. Narcissistic people have no empathy for others. They control, manipulate, gaslight, and use others to feed their ego. Other people's pain and attention are their narcissistic supply. Narcissistic parents often make their children become codependent or even narcissistic.

Now I've come to the realisation of what was wrong with my mum. I've learned the name of her psychological and mental illness. She was a narcissist, and I became codependent because of her. She didn't just give me traumas in my childhood; her trauma was still within me, and I was manifesting painful events and circumstances through that mindset and the traumas I developed in my childhood.

To heal, first, we need to recognise our emotional wounds and patterns and understand where they came from and validate our feelings. Knowing the emotional and psychological damage caused by my mum made me resent her more. For me, it was not difficult to forgive anyone except my mum. I tried to forgive her so many times, but I couldn't. I imagined her in front of me and told her so many times, "I forgive you, I set you free, and I set myself free," but it didn't work.

One part of me was happy with myself that at least I was validating my feelings. The culture I come from doesn't encourage talking about parental abuse and neglect. We are judged and classified as ungrateful if we speak out against our parents, especially our mothers.

We live in an illusionary society where mums are considered to be divas. We are reminded of their sacrifices and efforts they make for their children. We are told to be grateful for our parents, and there is no room to express the pain caused by them. Because of all these false ideas and programming, we can't see and validate our own emotional wounds and pain caused by our parents.

At least I was able to see reality as it is. At least I was brave enough to admit that my mum has caused me suffering and pain.

I completely stopped talking to my mum on the phone for a few years. The only person I had regular contact within Pakistan was my niece, Aqsa.

In the beginning, I never talked about my mum in front of my friends, neither in a good nor bad. Rajni's parents were very loving, and she always talked about them. She asked me once why I don't talk about my mum, and then I told her that my experience with my mum is not like yours. I told her everything about her. Even though her experience was different from mine, she understood me and didn't judge me for not liking my mum.

I read somewhere that forgiveness is a by-product of healing. When we understand how the universe works and heal ourselves, we automatically forgive our abuser. I made the decision to heal myself from all the emotional damage caused by my mum. I still wanted to forgive her by healing myself.

I was reading books and watching videos about codependency and narcissism. I was sharing that information and videos about codependency with Rajni. She never denied the information I was giving her but never fully grasped it either. She is the kind of person who takes time to accept and process new information. However, she says about me, "I am that kind of person; if I get to know something and it clicks, I will spend all my energy and time working on it, even if it's difficult or painful to accept and work on it." That's how we are, and we accept and respect the differences in our personalities.

I knew Rajni was also suffering because of her codependency, but I never tried to force her to change or heal. I was sharing my information with her but letting her process things in her own space.

I also came to the realisation that I am not just codependent; I am an empath. Empaths are sensitive people gifted at reading, detecting, and processing the energy around them. They can also absorb other people's energy and emotions as their own, which can be overwhelming and painful if the empath is not empowered and doesn't know how to use their gifts. Empaths are also sensitive to the spirit world and can feel and talk to spirits.

An empowered empath uses their gifts to feel others' pain, help them, and heal them. But when an empath is not healed and not in their power, that very gift can turn into a nightmare.

Now I came to understand why I was absorbing Ama's emotions and negative energy. I was an unhealed empath and didn't know how not to get affected by others' emotions and dense energy.

A question arose in my mind: I was not like that in Pakistan, and I got the answer. I grew up in a very painful environment, so I shut myself. Unconsciously, I created a strong shield around me and around my heart to protect myself. That shield was broken by Nafees, and my empathy abilities came to the surface, but I had no idea how to survive as an empath.

After coming to the realisation that I am an empath, I still didn't have the skills to thrive as an empath for many years. It took me so many years to become an empowered empath.

I hired two girls in my salon, and one of them had dense negative energy which I didn't know at that time. I was getting affected by her negative energy, and coming into contact with different clients with different energies every day was draining for me as an empath.

I kept working on my personal growth with my busy life, with business, and with three kids. I didn't try to bypass any dense emotions. I felt pain at its fullest and didn't try to run away from any uncomfortable feelings. It took me so many months to recover from my breakup with Haris.

He was regularly coming to pick up Talal every weekend. Co-parenting Talal with him had never been a problem. He loves Talal and looks after him very well. Witnessing him as a good dad earned my respect again. For the first few months, I didn't talk to him when he came to pick up and drop Talal; then slowly, we started talking. He talked respectfully with me, and now he started showing respect to my other two kids. I knew from the deepest corner of my heart that my relationship with him is over, and I will never get back to him again. However, I welcomed him back into my life as a friend, and he was happy to be my friend.

The building where I had my salon was on lease, and maintenance was my responsibility. I couldn't afford maintenance of the building, so I asked Haris if he could help, and he always helped me whenever I needed any maintenance job in my salon and in my home.

Because I didn't have any family, brother, or cousin in the UK, and I didn't drive, it was not easy for me to take the kids out. If I asked him if I wanted to take the kids out, he said yes. He was good with my other two kids now, and Aneeq still calls him daddy and shows Haris his affection and love.

I finished all my expectations and attachments with Haris. I was happy to receive whatever he was offering me as a friend, but I didn't have any expectations from him. In fact, I was not expecting to be his friend, but that happened automatically. I realised we were not compatible as romantic partners, but we were good as friends. We laughed, we joked, and could talk for hours, confusing people around us about our friendship.

In the culture we came from, it's not common to be friends with your ex. After divorce, people try to prove that it's not their fault, and it was the other partner who is completely responsible for what happened. I realised it's not about being wrong or right; we all try our best to the level of our understanding. Watching me and Haris as friends, people in our community were surprised and suspicious; however, I didn't care what they were thinking.

It was January 2019 when one day I woke up and found out my religious beliefs were washed away like someone pressed the delete button overnight. I was surprised to see my new self. I felt free. Glimpses of true freedom touched my awareness.

I had been told to believe certain ideas about God and been afraid to even question. As my religious beliefs washed away, I started questioning everything I had been told to believe. Those beliefs had kept me in a box all my life. We had also been given a belief that what I believe is right and what others believe is wrong. With my religious beliefs, that belief about wrong and right also washed away. This strengthened my understanding that nobody is wrong or right. We are all at different levels of evolution, and nobody has the right to judge anybody. People in this world need love, unity, and acceptance, not separation and judgment.

The feeling of not belonging to any specific group or judgmental God was giving me wings of freedom and transformation. The idea that God doesn't judge me and loves me unconditionally was the most comforting feeling, as Jesus said, "God is love".

I was moving from separate consciousness to unity consciousness. Coming to realisations that we all came from one source, and we are all connected to each other.

My love and connection with God started to grow more. I wanted to experience God directly, as I heard God lives within my heart, but my mind was dragging towards something else.

Slowly, my business and success started becoming my obsession. I wanted to be successful. I started learning about manifestation. I began making YouTube videos about makeup and hair. I created a vision board for my success. It was all about success as a salon owner, a makeup artist, and a hairdresser.

I started getting tired from working so hard, and as an empath, I was struggling and felt like dragging myself every day. My body started giving up. Some days I had no energy in my body; it was hard to even get out of bed, but my mind was forcing me to hold on to the idea of success and keep going no matter what.

I was working full-time as a hairdresser and makeup artist, looking after my staff, business, and three kids, and making YouTube videos, and I didn't have enough energy to do all these things. My body was telling me something else, and my mind was telling me to be successful no matter what. I was listening to my mind. I was watching YouTube videos about success, money, and manifestation alongside codependency, narcissism, hair, and makeup. I was pushing myself so hard, and whatever I was doing, nothing was working. I was feeling stuck, exhausted, stressed, and helpless.

During all this, Rajni's dad died. It was almost a year, but she was still grieving. She was very close to her dad, and she was heartbroken by his death. I didn't want to bother her by telling her about my struggle.

One day I came upstairs from work, and I told the kids I am going to my room as I needed rest and please don't come to my room. I was tired, done with my struggle. I went to my room and started praying to God. I cried for several minutes and asked for help. I asked God again, I don't know what I am doing, something is missing, and I do not know what. Please help, I am open to receiving help.

I felt better after my prayer. The next day, a video showed up about mindfulness meditation. I had done six phase meditation in the past but had never heard about meditation with deep breathing. I started doing meditation. I felt like every deep breath was taking my stress and exhaustion away. Meditation was connecting me with my body, heart, and soul. Now I realised it was meditation which was missing in my life and what I really needed to relax and listen to my own self.

In the next few days, a book named "Conversations with God" came into my mind, like someone was whispering this name in my ear to read this book. I had heard this book's name once, three years ago, but never thought to buy it. But now, after three years, I felt like I was being told to read this book. I even remembered the name of the writer, Neale Donald Walsch. I ordered the book "Conversations with God" as the name of the book was inspiring for me. I always believed in prayers but never thought we can have conversations with God.

The writer, Neale Donald Walsch, was struggling in life, and he decided to write a letter to God that led him to have a conversation with God. He asked questions about relationships, money, sex, and the struggle of humanity, and he got the answers. Answers that I was seeking.

As soon as I started reading that book, something started shifting in me. That book is not just a book; it has energy in it. The book breathes and feels alive, which can change your being if you allow it. I was tired of my struggle, so I allowed this new information and energy to penetrate me. I read in "Conversations with God", "observe your feelings, thoughts, and actions". I started observing myself without judgment.

I had the realisation that I got stuck in my ego. After my awakening when I started working on myself, my ego felt threatened, and it came online with its full force. My ego held onto the idea of success, and it was telling me to show the world that I matter by showing my success. My ego wants to compensate for my two failed marriages with my salon success, and I got stuck in my ego.

Spiritually, after my awakening, I was facing what spiritual teachers call the dark night of the soul. Meditation, Awakening, and healing are the death of the ego, and the ego doesn't like to die. Before the ego dies, it gives a more difficult time for its survival, but when the ego reaches its peak and life doesn't work according to the plans of the ego, it dies on its own accord.

That's happened to me: my ego was making plans for my success that were not aligned with my soul's plans. Because it was not aligned with my soul, I was tired, exhausted, and stressed. Mindfulness meditation and the book "Conversations with God" helped me to surrender my ego and get aligned with my soul. My ego didn't die, but it loosened its control over my life. As my ego loosened its control, I started listening to my higher self and developed a connection with my inner guide. I began listening to my intuition rather than my ego mind.

I felt like I had another awakening. I had self-realisation this time. I deeply knew that "I know nothing." What a great start to the journey of knowing myself and the universe. There is a difference between knowledge and knowing. I had been given knowledge about God, the universe, and how things work, and most of it was false knowledge. That knowledge gives the illusion of knowing but not true knowing. Knowledge is borrowed, and knowing is a direct experience from your heart, soul, and source. False knowledge becomes a barrier to knowing the truth, and I made the decision to know the truth. To know the truth, I had to drop the old knowledge. As soon as I dropped the old knowledge, only one knowing was left: I knew nothing.

It was November 2019, as my ego surrendered a bit, I saw my vision board and had a deep realisation: that's not what my soul wants in this lifetime. Success as a salon owner was not what my soul wanted, and my soul had different life plans. My higher self whispered new goals in my ear, and I started listening to my higher self without any resistance. I began changing my vision board. My higher self whispered "bestseller book" on my vision board. I listened to my higher self, and my mind was telling me that I am a hairdresser, and how on earth will I write a bestseller book? I didn't even have an idea about what I would write a book about, but after a few weeks, I had the intuition that I would write an autobiography. However, I didn't think too much about the book at that time except for putting a picture of a bestseller book on my vision board.

I put pictures of my dream house, my dream car, my dream holidays, my dream man, and my dream bank balance. I had heard about enlightenment, and I wrote "enlightenment" on my vision board without knowing what enlightenment is. I always wanted to have the best relationship with my kids, so I wrote "wonderful relationships with kids." I had the intuition that I would be a spiritual life coach, so I set goals as a spiritual life coach. I wrote a few affirmations on my vision board:

- I am loveable.

- I believe in myself.

- I believe in my soul.

- I earn millions.

- I am a millionaire.

When I saw my new vision board, my mind cringed and asked me if I was worthy to receive all these. Was I someone who could cherish such achievements? Did I even have it in me to chase such dreams? During such moments of self-doubt, I actively started reminding my mind that I am worthy to receive all these. I didn't have an idea when I would write a book and manifest my dreams, but I knew that to manifest my dreams I needed to get alignment with my mind, body, and soul, and to get alignment I needed to heal myself and raise my vibrations. I knew that to heal myself it might take years, so I wasn't attached to my goals. I made the vision board, put my desire into the universe, and then forgot about it and started my spiritual healing journey.

My friend Rajni was going through a lot in her life. She was at her lowest point in her life. After reading the book "Conversations with God," I gave this book to Rajni and I told her this book helped me a lot and it can also help you. I also told her about mindfulness meditation. This time she listened to me. She started meditating every day and started reading the book. In the next few weeks, Rajni had her spiritual awakening. She told me meditation was helping her to take her stress and worries away. The book "Conversations with God" opened her eyes and touched her heart. She seriously started working on herself and she never stopped meditating since she started, just like me. She started feeling good and stopped taking sleeping pills which she had been taking for almost a decade. She told me she doesn't need sleeping pills as she is sleeping well since she is doing meditation. I was happy for Rajni; finally, she started her healing journey.

I was still very busy in my business and life was like a hamster on a wheel for me. In December 2019, after Christmas, I had a cold and flu and a high temperature so bad that I could not go to work for a few days. That was my first break from work in about two years. I could not do anything except lying on the couch with a fever. My body and my mind needed that break. During that break, I watched my kids for twenty-four hours and realised that my kids needed me more than anything else in the world. That sickness helped me to rest and gain clarity in thinking about my life. I made the decision to sell my salon.

Just meditation is not enough to gain clarity. Our whole lifestyle matters. When we are extra busy in life chasing things like a hamster in a hamster wheel, we don't get a chance to relax and review our lives and the mistakes we are making. A break is needed to watch our actions and realise where we are trying to go by running and chasing things that may not be aligned with our soul, and it could be draining our life energy in the wrong direction.

I am grateful that the universe gave me a break by making me sick so I could make one of the best decisions of my life. When I told my friends about my decision to sell the salon, they were all shocked including Rajni. My friends knew how ambitious I was about my business. For them, I was giving up on my dreams, but in reality, I was not giving up on my dreams; I was following my new dreams which were aligned with my renewed soul purpose – this included a healed purpose of life and dreams which even my physical mind had never imagined in its wildest dreams.

My friends asked me what I would do after selling that salon, but I couldn't offer them an answer; I had no idea myself as of yet. I told them I might work as a mobile hairdresser, I might work from home or rent a chair but I had no clear plan what I will do after selling the salon. Selling the salon was another leap of faith.

It was January 2020 when a spiritual woman came to my salon. She told me she is into spirituality and meditation for thirty years. I was new to spirituality, so I was very excited to meet her and got very much fascinated by her wisdom spiritual insights. She suddenly told me that the universe will send a man into my life who will love me, and I will have a beautiful relationship with him. I knew intuitively that that is not her who is telling me, it's the source, who was letting me know through her. But the question drumming in my mind was: why the source wants me to know this? I only realised this after a few years.

I had three girls working in my salon and two already left. One girl who I thought I could trust her also left suddenly without giving any notice when she got to know that I was selling the salon.

I had a big salon where I was working all by myself. I was doing everything I could to keep the business running alongside looking after my kids and working on my healing. I was also taking driving lessons. Healing also can be tiring for our body and as a non-empowered empath meeting with lots of people and working too much more than my capacity was exhausting for me. I wanted to sell the salon as soon as possible. The urgency was demanding and intense.

Lockdown for rising up.

I passed my driving test and bought my first car in March 2020. After two days of buying a car, lockdown happened. My body and my mind really needed a break, and I got that break in lockdown. That lockdown proved to be a blessing for me. I had the time to spend with my kids and explore spirituality more. Rajni and I started doing meditation for one hour.

I read the entire series of "Conversations with God" and all the other works of Neal Donald Walsch. I read the book "Angels in My Hair" by Lorna Byrne and came to know that we all have guardian angels who love us unconditionally and comfort us in times of need whether we know it or not. I read Dr Brian Weiss's book "Many Lives, Many Masters" and his other books as well. I came to know that we all have spirit guides, and we are loved and guided throughout our life journey. Exact information and books were showing up in my life which I needed to know.

Rajni and I were enjoying meditation and reading books in lockdown, and we were talking on the phone every day for hours. Rajni was getting very good at meditation, and she started going deep into the thoughtless stage in her meditation. She also started seeing visions in her meditation. We both were very fascinated and surprised by our spiritual experiences.

She rang me one day and told me that she saw a vision that I was with a little four- or five-year-old girl and she was my daughter. I was surprised to know that as I never thought about having another child. I told her that might be my Mr Right's girl and if he has a daughter, that would be nice. I would love her as my own daughter as I missed not having a daughter.

Rajni had another vision. She was shown four demons and told we needed to work on them. The four demons were:

1. ego
2. fear
3. attachments
4. anger

Rajni told me this vision was for both of us and we need to work on it. I realised we all need to work on these four demons and this vision was for everyone. We both never forgot that vision and kept working on these four demons.

Kundalini Awakening

One day, Rajni told me that she is feeling a certain energy around her spine which makes her body move in her meditation. Rajni and I were sharing our spiritual information with each other. One day she sent me a video about six stages of spiritual awakening by Christina Lopes. After watching that video, I came to know that what was happening to us was called spiritual awakening. After watching that video, another video showed up about Kundalini awakening. I had never heard of Kundalini awakening before, but that name just clicked with me.

I watched that video and found out Rajni was having a Kundalini awakening. I sent Rajni that video and it helped her to know what was happening to her. Rajni and I watched all Christina Lopes's videos and she became our favourite spiritual teacher.

Kundalini energy is a divine powerful healing energy that we all have. It's housed at the base of your spine and when it's awakened, it travels up the spinal column and activates the seven chakras. Kundalini is also the process of purification of our bodies and psyche and causes us to transform on all levels. I did my research about Kundalini energy after Rajni's awakening but I didn't expect my own Kundalini awakening until it happened one day.

I was sitting in meditation when I noticed an energy in my lower back rising and my body started moving back and forth. For the next few days, I felt a warm energy in my lower back going slowly up. Then, one day I was meditating when I saw a vision in my meditation. I saw myself as a very dirty person; someone who hadn't showered for a prolonged time and didn't change clothes for years. When I came out of deep meditation, I didn't understand what was being shown to me. Then my body started shaking and moving. Kundalini energy which I was feeling in my lower spine started moving all over my body, especially in my chakras.

When my body started moving too much, I had the intuition to stand up. Upon standing up and letting my body relax, it began assuming different yoga poses. Despite never having practised yoga before and lacking knowledge of any poses, I recognised that I was indeed doing yoga. At times, my hands would form an energy ball, which I would then automatically send to all my chakras. The vision of myself appearing dirty suddenly made sense to me. It dawned on me that the shame, fear, guilt, and wounded energy within me were lowering my vibration and frequency.

As the Kundalini energy worked to purify me, it cleaned up my chakras and dissolved all the denser, wounded energy. Rajni and I shared some similarities in our experiences of Kundalini awakening, although there were notable differences. While her energy predominantly moved towards her third eye chakra, mine primarily focused on my lower chakras initially. Our shared experiences guided us towards the right information through books and videos, reassuring us that we were not going insane.

Following my second awakening, I established a connection with my higher self and became more adept at listening to my intuition. I intuitively knew that everything was unfolding for my highest good. Due to the lockdown, I found myself free and brimming with energy, making it the opportune time for healing and Kundalini awakening.

Sometimes, my body would engage in one-hour movement sessions both in the morning and evening. I ceased feeling drained and exhausted, instead feeling invigorated and capable of performing the necessary body movements to clear all dense energy.

Death of Ego

One night, as I slept, I observed a ball of energy rising from the base of my spine and ascending to my forehead with intense pressure.

Although asleep, a part of me remained aware of this energy movement. Upon the ball of energy emerging from my forehead with force, I woke up feeling surprised and confused by the experience. In the following days, I experienced a sensation akin to dying one afternoon, leaving me feeling bewildered and unsure of what to do.

My son Aneeq attempted to converse with me, and in my state, I expressed to him that I felt like I was dying. Initially frightened, he later understood and gave me the space I needed to process. Upon introspection, I intuitively realised that it was not my physical self but rather my ego that was undergoing a form of death. This experience of ego death, albeit brief, revealed how closely we identify with our ego, to the extent that its dissolution can resemble real death. Following the death of my ego, my higher self assumed control, although remnants of my ego remained. Now, my ego operated subtly, allowing me to observe its presence and choose whether to react through ego or respond through conscious awareness. Previous attempts to heal my codependency on a purely psychological level had proven ineffective. However, delving into spirituality and experiencing the death of my ego enabled me to develop compassion for others. Embracing the notion that "I have sent you nothing but angels" from "Conversations with God," I began seeing angelic aspects in everyone who entered my life, recognising them as messengers sent by the divine.

Even challenging individuals served as valuable teachers, contributing to my personal growth. This realisation highlighted the intricate nature of reality, where there are no heroes or villains, but rather co-creators shaping their realities.

Joining the Third Person

Rajni had a vision indicating that another individual would join us on our spiritual journey. While she did not discern a face, she saw the presence of a third person accompanying us. Speculating on the identity of this person within our circle, I received a call one day from a client named Iram. Despite not having spoken to her during the lockdown or mentioned Kundalini energy, Iram expressed an interest in meditation. Due to lockdown restrictions, we decided to meet in a park, where I instructed her in meditation. Later that evening, she contacted me to share her meditation experience, describing sensations of energy rising along her spine and culminating in her head, resulting in movement. This revelation confirmed to me that she, too, was undergoing a Kundalini awakening.

Iram was a very reserved person with a strong emotional barrier, so I wasn't particularly close to her. Nevertheless, whenever we met, I would share my spiritual insights with her. While she didn't embrace spirituality and healing to the extent Rajni and I did, her Kundalini was still working to heal her, despite her irregular meditation practice.

I Saw Energy

During lockdown, on a bright sunny day in the park, as I lay on the grass watching the beautiful sky while the kids played, I observed Earth's energy with my naked eyes. It appeared as thin, transparent wires connecting with each other in a network of dots, vibrating in unison. I was mesmerised by the sight and kept staring at the energy until my kids interrupted me. Coming out of lockdown I underwent a significant transformation and emerged with newfound energy. I utilised this time for healing, reading books, watching YouTube videos, and spending time with my kids.

After three months, my Kundalini energy calmed down and began focusing primarily on my heart chakra. Whenever I relaxed, I could feel the energy on my heart, cleansing and opening my heart chakra. When Kundalini energy was active, my chest would move in and out, but this only occurred when I was alone and relaxed, never in public or in someone's presence.

After lockdown, I reopened my salon while still attempting to sell my business. Eventually, my salon sold in September 2020. The building's lease was to be transferred to the new owner, so I needed to vacate the flat above the salon by the end of September. Desiring a house with a backyard for my kids, I found that the rental rates in the areas I was considering were too high. I prayed to God and my angels, specifying my requirements for a house: a garden and an extra small room where I could set up my salon, all for £600 rent.

One of my clients informed me that her cousin had purchased a new house adjacent to theirs, which they were renovating and seeking tenants for. Although they had received offers of £900 rent, I asked if they would consider renting it to me for £600. To my delight, they agreed, and I went to view the house with Rajni.

It matched exactly what I had requested from my angels and God: a three-bedroom house with a large backyard and an additional small room for my salon, all at the rent I desired. I loved the house and moved in on 30th September 2020. It had been renovated with new carpeting, a kitchen, and flooring.

Talal's father assisted me with the move. I purchased new furniture and decorated it to my liking, deciding to give working from home as a hairdresser a chance, as it would be more convenient with the kids. I had no expectations about how it would turn out financially, but Rajni believed in me, assuring me that I would succeed.

Haris renovated a small room for my salon, and my small business began to thrive. My kids were delighted to have me home all the time, and I started taking them out regularly. Talal started full-time primary school, while Raham began high school, making good friends, including one best friend. My bond with the kids deepened over time. I began taking Raham for breakfast and walks during his school breaks, which strengthened our connection. I hadn't previously had a strong, deep connection with my kids. Despite my efforts to be a good mother, I was unsure how to connect with them as I was disconnected from myself. I came to realise that we cannot form deep connections with others when we are disconnected from ourselves and feeling lost.

As I connected more with my higher self, my bond with my kids deepened. Achieving a wonderful relationship with my kids, as per the first goal on my vision board, was a significant milestone. I advised Talal's father not to shout at Talal, but to show him love and make him feel safe and valued. He heeded my advice, never raising his voice in Talal's presence. Talal is a happy and joyful child, and parenting him has been easy and enjoyable. I refrain from shouting at Talal, respecting his opinions and individuality. I adhered to my spiritual practices and morning routine, waking up at 5 a.m. to exercise for 45 minutes, meditate for another 45 minutes, recite my daily affirmations, and shower. After completing my morning routine, I'd wake up the kids for school.

Following my separation from Haris, I refrained from dating or seeking a partner for two and a half years. However, I began the search for the love of my life. My perspective on marriage had evolved, and I was now clear that I didn't want to marry just for the sake of it or to avoid loneliness. I realised that marriage without love is merely a contractual arrangement, often used for control or to fulfill societal norms. Instead, I sought genuine love and connection in any future relationship.

I was not against marriage. I longed to marry the love of my life. I just believed that if marriage is a union of two open-hearted and healed souls, then it's beautiful, but if it's merely a contract to control the other person and share wounds and misery, then it's ugly.

I made the decision to find the love of my life with whom I can share my love and my soul because I deserve love. To find the love of my life, I was willing to heal my broken heart and work to clear all the blocks that were hindering me from attracting romantic love into my life.

From the background I came from, we were conditioned to spend our lives with one person without questions, whether our parents chose them for us or we chose them ourselves. We were told to tolerate bad behaviour and stay with that person until death, even if we didn't feel loved, cared for, appreciated, or valued. I was letting go of the old templates from my mind that had never served me.

Dating and finding love were new worlds for me, and I had no idea how the dating life worked. I started learning about dating by watching videos of dating coaches. I wasn't afraid to learn new skills. I learned what to expect on dates, how high-value women behave, and what red flags to watch out for in men. I downloaded a dating app and started going on dates. I found out that dating is a whole new world, and finding the love of your life is not easy when you still have so many unhealed traumas and wounds to work on. I didn't know all my blocks and wounds, but I knew that if I wasn't attracting love, it meant I wasn't ready yet, and I needed to keep working on myself. When I would be ready, and my divine time would come, the universe would send him into my life.

Rajni's psychic abilities were improving over time. We found out that she had the soul gift to receive messages from angels and spirit guides and communicate with the spirit world. She communicated with her dad's spirit and a few other spirits of departed loved ones in her family. The spirits world sometimes speak in symbols and images, and she was learning the language of the spirit world and how to interpret it.

Sometimes she just saw the vision and didn't know the meaning, and when she described her vision to me, I interpreted it with my intuitive skills and inner guidance. Rajni heard a man's name, including his surname, in her deep meditation. She told me she heard the name very clearly three times and had no idea who he was. I told her that it might be the name of the love of my life.

Rajni and I found out that we are lightworker souls. A lightworker soul is a soul that spreads light and comes to this earth with a service mission to the planet. Earth is going through a major transformation, and millions of lightworker souls have come, and more are still coming, with a service mission to help humanity in their healing and evolution. To spread light and help others in their healing, Rajni and I needed to work on our own shadows, come into the light, and then hold that light for others.

There are many types of lightworker souls, and Rajni and I are still learning what our soul's gifts are and how we can help humanity and the planet Earth with our unique soul's gift and service mission.

She told me in the summer of 2021 that she saw a vision for us in her deep meditation. She saw three tunnels. One tunnel represented me. That tunnel was not completely dark; there was a dim light in it, allowing you to still see things. Then I took a right turn, and there was light. The second tunnel represented her. There was still very dim light, but not as in the first tunnel. She was still walking in the tunnel, and after much walking, there was light. Then there was a third tunnel, which represented my friend Iram. In that tunnel, there was only darkness, and this tunnel led nowhere.

What we gathered from that vision was that something would happen in my life that would lead me to take a right turn, and that right turn would lead me to the light. Rajni's tunnel showed that she would reach the light slowly, and it would take time. The darkness of Iram's tunnel was already apparent because she was not doing anything for her healing except experiencing a Kundalini awakening. Would she reach the light in this lifetime? I had no idea. Rajni saw another vision for me following that vision. She saw my life as a boat first, then it turned into a train, and then aeroplanes. I understood the message that was being shown to her. My life in Pakistan was like being in a boat, slow. When I came to the UK, my life gained speed like a train, with shaking and lots of movement. Then my life was going to be like an aeroplane, fast and smooth.

Rajni saw another vision in which she saw four spiritual chairs. On three of them were Rajni, Iram, and me. There was someone on the fourth chair whom she didn't know, and their face was not shown.

I met a Pakistani guy, Rohan, on a dating app. He was two years younger than me. When he rang me on the phone for the first time, we spoke for two hours. It was very easy to talk to him; he was very friendly. From our initial talk, I realised we were not compatible as romantic partners. So, when we decided to meet, I told him to come and see me as a friend, and not to think of it as a date. He was okay with that.

We decided to meet at a café in the park for breakfast and then go for a walk. I arrived first and was waiting for him at the café door. He approached me with open arms, gave me a big hug, and brought flowers and chocolates.

We had breakfast and a good conversation. He opened up easily and told me about his childhood, marriage, and divorce. He has kids who live with their mum and visit him every two weeks. He told me that he had a difficult childhood and his dad left them suddenly when he was five years old.

My skill in reading others' energy, beliefs, and traumas was improving. I could clearly feel and see that he was an empath and codependent, like a male version of Rajni and me. I told him that he was an empath and codependent, and that he needed to heal himself; otherwise, he would suffer more in life as an unhealed empath and codependent. He seemed okay with accepting that he was an empath, but accepting codependency was hard for his ego mind. I also noticed he had a fear of abandonment and a strong belief that his loved ones would leave him. I told him about his beliefs and informed him that he would manifest people leaving him, especially his romantic partner, because of his beliefs. He told me that his wife left him a few years ago. I taught him meditation, but he didn't seem interested in doing it, and I wasn't interested in noticing that he wasn't interested. His pain reminded me of my own pain, and I just wanted to rescue him.

We spent three hours together, and it was the first time I spent that much time with a man I went to see. We had a good time together. I felt comfortable and at home with him. However, there was not any romantic attraction on either side, and we decided to become friends.

I had the intuition that we were meant to be friends and that he was the fourth person who was sitting in that spiritual chair. I told him about Rajni's vision, but he couldn't grasp it and kind of disbelieved it.

Rohan and I started talking on the phone regularly. I found out he was a different type of man from the ones I had known so far. He had a soft heart because he was an empath. He was sensitive, talkative, friendly, cheeky, open-minded, and had a good sense of humour. I enjoyed talking to him. I invited him to my house, and he was genuinely good and friendly with my kids, who fell in love with him.

Rohan told me on the phone that he was having a nap one afternoon when he noticed a strong and intense ball rising from his spine and coming out from his forehead with full force, and he got up because of that. I told him I had a similar experience in lockdown. I hadn't told him that before, and I knew what he experienced.

He was doing his master's degree in IT and was living in a hostel in Manchester. He invited me to Manchester. I went to see him by train, and he picked me up from the train station. We went to his hostel as his sister was coming to see me there, and she was bringing lunch for me, which she had cooked. Rohan and I were waiting for his sister in his hostel room, and my mind was wondering if he might do something. Thoughts were rushing through my mind about how I could trust this guy and sit in his room alone. However, I didn't notice any weird signs or any red flags from him. We watched TV and talked until his sister arrived. We had lunch together with his sister. He dropped his sister off at her work, and we went to the park after a walk. He loved photography and did a photoshoot of me in the park. When I was sitting on the train to come back home, he was standing on the station near my train. There was a quote written on the station wall: "There is always a person who cares about you." When I read that quote, I pointed it out to him and gave him a sign from my train window that I would be that person who cares about him. He had a big smile on his face and said thank you.

I was mesmerised by my experience with him, and we became best friends. It felt like I found another member of my soul family. I introduced him to Rajni, Iram, and other friends, including Haris. Rohan also introduced me to his friends and family very proudly, as if he felt proud to be my friend.

One of my friends told me that Rohan and I get along very well and we might develop romantic feelings later. I told her that I am crystal clear we will never have a romantic relationship, as my inner guide told me.

I was also crystal clear about what I want in my romantic partner. I wanted a man who is already awakened, healed, and in his healed masculine energy. Who is emotionally mature and knows how to regulate his emotions. Who knows himself and his self-worth. Who knows how to love, treat, and respect women, and with whom I can have a sacred partnership.

Despite Rohan's good nature and connection with him, I knew that he was not emotionally mature. He was not over his ex and had so much to heal. If I find any man who is wounded and needs my help, I would friendzone him and help him to heal if he wants my help. But I was determined not to choose a wounded man as my romantic partner whom I must rescue and parent.

Rohan started dating a girl whom he brought to my house once. He broke up with that girl in a few weeks and started talking to another girl. We used to tell each other everything about our dates. He stopped talking to the new girl in a few weeks and was feeling very low. He told me that he feels lonely, and I also noticed that he had depression. He asked me if he could come to my house to stay for a few days.

I knew how it feels to be lonely and depressed and wanted to help him to help himself, so I said yes. He stayed one week in my house. He was working in an IT company and used to work from home. Rohan loves kids, and my kids were having a great time with him. I noticed that something was going on in Rohan's mind. He started having romantic feelings for me.

One morning, when I went to the bedroom where he was sleeping to ask him if he wants breakfast, I noticed he looked stunned. I asked him what happened, and he told me he had a dream. In his dream, he was asking a spirit or spiritual figure if he could have a romantic relationship with me, and that spirit said firmly no. "You cannot have a romantic relationship with her, and you guys will always be friends."

He also told me he woke up after that dream and noticed a spirit in the room, and because he was not spiritual and had no idea how the spirit world works, he got frightened. He didn't have any idea how strong and powerful we humans are, and there was nothing to be frightened of.

I told him that I already knew we would never have a romantic relationship, so it's better to get that out of your mind. I used to cook his favourite foods for him and pampered him, which he loved.

When he went back, my kids started asking when he is coming back to stay again. He came back to stay for a week again after one month. This time, in my house, he saw a dream. In his dream, he saw four spiritual persons. He was one of them, and another was me. The other two he couldn't see their faces. When he told me about that dream, I reminded him of Rajni's vision and told him that the other two were Rajni and Iram.

He was still in disbelief that he could be the fourth spiritual person in our group. Despite his dream about me, and me making sure he understands we are not compatible for a romantic relationship, he was still romanticising me in his mind and started having infatuation. I knew that his feelings were temporary, it would go away, and I didn't take his feelings seriously.

He was having spiritual experiences, and I knew from the deep core of my heart that he had his calling for awakening, but he was not listening to his soul. When Rajni and I had our calling for awakening, we grabbed it and even got attached to it in the beginning. Rohan and Iram, on the other hand, were resisting their awakening and the new and better version of themselves, which was waiting for them. They were so attached to their old self and their old identity that they didn't want to let go of their old self and ego despite their suffering in life.

Rajni and I started judging them for their resistance to healing, and Rajni got the message in her meditation that all four spiritual people sitting in those spiritual chairs would reach the light. Rajni and I stopped judging them and started trying to understand that we are all different and we all have our unique ways of healing and dealing with our shadows, and everything happens in divine time.

I was not affected by Rohan's temporary feelings and infatuation and didn't let it affect our friendship. He finished his master's degree and was meant to move out from the university hostel. He bought a house in another city, and I helped with his deposit for his house.

My son Raham was approaching his teenage years and growing into an intelligent and smart young man. Because of his bossy nature, he was the man of the house. I was adaptable by nature, so I was okay with being dominated by him sometimes. I was happy that thalassemia didn't affect his life and he had hundred percent attendance in his Year 7 of high school.

With my kids, good friends, a solid social circle, and a thriving business, we were having the best period of our lives. I felt blessed and grateful for life. I started enjoying music and going for regular walks in nature, feeling deeply connected to it.

I was on cloud nine and didn't know that it was time to come down and face that darkness again.

Chapter 7 – Tour to the Dark Tunnel

March 1st, 2022. That day is etched in my memory forever. It was Raham's 13th birthday, a day I thought would be filled with joy. I looked forward to seeing my son become a teenager, thinking it would mean less worry for me as he grew up. But life had other plans.

On the morning of his birthday, I went to Raham's room as usual to wake him up and wish him happy birthday. But something was off. He said he wasn't feeling well and showed me a swollen lymph node on his neck. Touching him, I realised he had a fever. I decided to keep him home from school and took him to the doctor. The doctor said he had a lymph node infection and gave him antibiotics. But even after a week, he didn't get better.

We went back to the doctor, then to the hospital, but nothing seemed to help. Raham was getting worse. He was weak, hardly eating, and spending most of his time in bed. I worried that his thalassemia might be worsening, but the doctor said it was stable. Still, Raham refused a blood transfusion.

During this time, my friend Rajni had a vision about Raham needing hospitalisation. And then Raham's behaviour started to change. He began talking to his teddy bears as if they were real, and he became paranoid, even hallucinating. He turned against my friend Rohan for no reason, which was strange as he was very fond of him, but his personality seemed to shift.

I knew something wasn't right. It wasn't just his physical health; something was going on in his mind too. I told the doctor about his mental health issues alongside his other symptoms, and they decided to admit him to the hospital for more tests.

I had to figure out what to do with my other kids while Raham was in hospital. I asked Rohan for help, and he agreed. The hospital said I could go home at night, and the nurses would look after Raham. I reasoned with my situation as a single mother who couldn't leave her young kids behind at home for nights, it was a relief when the staff agreed to take charge in taking care of my son, but I still worried about my kids and how they were coping.

Through all this, Raham's resistance to treatment only made things harder. His behaviour became even more erratic, and I just wanted to find out what was wrong and help him get better.

Doctors suspected he might have brain inflammation. They gave him antibiotics through an IV and conducted various tests including blood tests, MRI, EEG, lumbar puncture, and a lymph node biopsy.

Because of his mental health issues, they gave him a separate room. I stayed with him all day, but he shouted at me almost constantly. He swore at me, tried to hit me, and threw things like shoes, cups, and glasses. I had to be very careful to protect myself.

He kept saying he hated me and blamed me for being in the hospital. He even resisted sleep, fearing the doctors might give him a blood transfusion.

His behaviour was distressing, and I didn't know what serious illness he might have. It reminded me of my own childhood when my mum used to shout all day. I never expected my own son to have such serious mental health issues. His sudden change in mental and physical health shocked me, and I felt like I was sinking into darkness again.

In just a few weeks, I went from cloud nine to a dark tunnel. I tried to stay calm and strong, but it was overwhelming.

During an MRI, he threw a bottle of coke at me, causing me emotional and physical pain. A nurse showed compassion and advised me to rest in the parents' room.

I had intuition that, he would never be the same again. When Rajni called, I explained his behaviour, but she tried to reassure me that he would be fine after treatment. But I knew deep down that he wouldn't.

I realised this was the turn Rajni saw in her meditation for me. I had no idea how many more twists and turns awaited me.

When I came home, I couldn't hold back my tears. I didn't want my kids to see me upset. I went to toilet and cried for many minutes until I felt little better.

Raham's phone was with him in the hospital, and Rohan told me he was sending negative messages. I reminded Rohan that Raham wasn't himself and not to take it personally.

Raham said things to the nurses that didn't make sense, prompting them to call a social worker. A psychiatrist also assessed him for signs of autism, ADHD, and other mental disorders.

After nine days, Raham was discharged, but he had severe pain in his lower back from the lumbar puncture test. All his tests came back normal, but his health continued to decline. He couldn't take care of himself, and I had to brush his teeth and give him showers. His hair started falling out rapidly.

My heart ached seeing Raham in pain and losing his mind. He was physically present, but it felt like he wasn't there. I missed the old Raham, the smart and confident version of him with whom I used to have conversations. It was a profound loss; I felt like I had lost my healthy son.

He became violent, and I had to keep an eye on him to protect his brothers from his outbursts. Despite my efforts to create a peaceful home, chaos returned. I tried my best to shield my younger children from any trauma.

The doctor recommended steroid treatment, so Raham was hospitalised again. Rohan came to look after my younger children while I prepared to go to the hospital. Raham called me, stressed and demanding my immediate presence. Rohan judged me for showing my emotions, seeing it as a sign of weakness. He seemed oblivious to my struggles, lacking compassion or understanding.

I realised he believed showing dense emotions meant weakness, but I didn't confront him as I was already worried about Raham.

After three days in hospital, Raham returned home. His appetite improved, and his physical health slightly bettered, but his mental state remained unchanged. He couldn't even recognise his little brother Talal.

The day after Raham's return, I had a car accident. Though no one was hurt, it added to my burdens. Raham's illness seemed like more than enough trial; the accident felt like an extra blow.

Raham's memory started deteriorating, causing him to forget names, places, and childhood memories. It was heartbreaking to witness.

Meanwhile, Rohan's behaviour changed. He seemed disinterested in my struggles, focusing on someone else. Feeling abandoned by my supposed best friend hurt, but I stopped seeking his help or attention. I made it clear that he should only contact me when he genuinely wanted to talk.

He didn't understand, resorting to text messages instead of our usual phone calls. His messages felt insincere, like he was only reaching out out of obligation. Feeling disrespected, I told him to come back only when he truly needed a friend and blocked him.

I realised he was wounded and avoiding his own pain. Instead of seeking true connection, he sought distractions, failing to see my pain and struggles.

I understood why he acted that way, but it still broke my heart. I cried, but I made sure not to show my tears to him. I realised I wouldn't share my emotions with someone who didn't value them. Despite facing many challenges, a part of me remained strong and aware. I knew how to stand up for myself, and I didn't seek anything from those who couldn't offer emotional support, although I allowed myself to feel my emotions.

I became attached to him. I worked on handling my attachments by embracing them without fear but remaining flexible and easy-going. If I did get attached, I observed myself consciously and deeply understood my attachments, gradually releasing them.

It wasn't Rohan who hurt me; it was my attachments and expectations from him. I learned the lesson the universe wanted to teach me. I understood the difference between unconditional love and attachment. Attachment arises from selfishness, expecting others to behave as we want, leading to hurt when they don't meet our expectations.

Unconditional love, on the other hand, frees us from bondage, allowing us to love without expecting anything in return. It sets both parties free, whether they choose to stay with us or not. I was learning to love unconditionally, which required letting go of attachments, the hardest part being understanding and feeling them fully.

While looking after Raham and my other children, I allowed myself to experience all my intense emotions. Raham began trying to escape from home, fearing hospitalisation if I took him to his appointments. One night, the police called to inform me they had found him and were bringing him home from McDonald's. I hid the keys as advised by the police, feeling like I was walking on eggshells.

The sense of aliveness and cheerfulness faded away as I peeled another layer of healing, revealing a feeling of numbness inside me. I experienced continuous pain and sadness.

I stopped socialising with friends and going out for dinner, except with Rajni, who visited occasionally if I asked her to come. Her mother-in-law's arrival from India kept her busy with family matters.

One day, Raham managed to find the keys under my pillow while I was asleep and escaped from home again. When I woke up in the morning, he wasn't there, and I panicked, calling the police. They found him and brought him home.

Throughout the day, he was trying to run away, agitated, frustrated, and angry. Whenever I approached him, he'd say, "Get off me."

By the end of the day, I was physically and mentally exhausted. When I went to bed, Aneeq and Talal were restless in their room. I tried to settle them down, but I didn't have the energy. I broke down in front of them, crying. Talal came to me, hugged me, and reassured me, behaving beyond his years. He held my hand and said, "mama, sorry to annoy you. You don't worry, everything will be fine." I thanked him and returned to my room while they went to sleep. Those mere words were just the light I need to carry on during the darkest days of my life. Talal, being only six years old, was feeling all the heartache that my broken motherly heart was feeling.

Feeling guilty for crying in front of my kids, I felt emotionally weak and helpless. I prayed to God, expressing my exhaustion and frustration, feeling like I couldn't bear it anymore. I said with frustration "this trial is too much to handle I am done with my struggle, I am done"

When I met Rajni, I confided in her, feeling lost in the darkness. She empathised with me, offering hope that this trial would be my last. Her compassion gave me a glimmer of hope.

Rajni asked if she could help, but I felt that my pain was mine to bear alone. Talal's dad arrived to pick him up for the weekend, and as we were chatting, the police arrived. Raham had called them, alleging that I locked him up and refused to feed him. Rajni explained the situation to the police, highlighting Raham's mental health issues and medical condition.

One day, Raham attempted to run away again, demanding the keys and hitting me. He confessed to taking some tablets meant for my hay fever, and I immediately called for an ambulance. As the ambulance and police arrived, I felt like a failure as a mother, unable to protect my children. Failure as a mom was the least thing my ego could digest.

My neighbor came out from their houses to see why there is police car and ambulance in front of my house. In the ambulance, I battled with my ego, feeling judged by those around me. But my higher self reminded me that my worth wasn't defined by my circumstances. Despite the reassurance, Raham's agitation and anger continued to worry me on the way to the hospital.

Arriving at the hospital, I was still shaken. Thankfully, Raham showed no adverse effects from the tablets. The psychiatrist noticed my distress and acknowledged it, prompting tears to well up in my eyes. When she said, "I think you are shattered," what followed was the fastest "yes" that had ever left my mouth. It was that moment I realised I was, in all honesty, struggling beyond my comprehension and capability.

Raham was restless, agitated, and angry with me throughout our time in the hospital. They kept him overnight for observation, and we returned home in the morning.

With Rajni busy with her mother-in-law, I found myself without someone to confide in regularly. Some of my clients would ask me how I was feeling, and I shared my emotions with a few of them.

Previously, I used to teach my clients about personal growth and spirituality, guiding them through meditation and healing during challenging times. Now, I found myself in need of help, and some of my clients offered me emotional support and listened to me.

One night, I heard Raham crying out in pain. When I went to his room, I found him struggling to get up from the floor, his legs hurting so much he couldn't walk. He desperately needed to use the toilet but could hardly move. Seeing him like this, I panicked and started crying, feeling helpless.

Unable to decide what to do, I called a friend who lived nearby and asked her to come over. I was in tears as I explained the situation, unsure whether to call an ambulance. I didn't want to take Raham to the hospital unnecessarily, as I had no one to look after my other two children. I hoped she could help me figure out what to do.

As we sat together, both crying, Raham began to feel better. He went back to bed after using the toilet. When my friend left, she suggested that Raham might be pretending to be sick for attention and didn't have any real medical condition. Feeling shattered and vulnerable after witnessing my son struggling to do something so simple, I couldn't defend my son against her judgment.

I knew my son, and from the deep core of my heart, I knew he was not physically well and that something physical was causing his mental health issues, so I didn't buy what she said. Throughout Raham's illness, no matter what I was going through, one part of me inside always remained strong. That day, witnessing Raham crying in pain broke me into many pieces. She saw me shattered and vulnerable, so she got the courage to say that in front of me, that my son was pretending.

As she left, I started googling and found out he had legs cramped, which lasted a few minutes, one of the symptoms of brain inflammation.

I went to my friend's house the next day and told her that he was not pretending to get attention. I was composed and strong that day. Seeing me strong, she couldn't say anything and slowly she has accepted that he was really not well.

When I was living my best life, I made new friends. I invested in them, giving them my time, effort, and energy as I had enough to give. With no family in the UK, my friends were my family, but when I needed them in my time of need, people turned their backs, or maybe it was time to let go of my expectations.

I realised how difficult it could be to look after three kids, including one ill child, as a single mum with no family around. But one part of me was still determined that I would rather choose my struggle as a single mum than be in an unhealthy relationship.

Before I was awakened, I had too many expectations from people, even unrealistic ones. Now I had the realisation that nobody can take away my suffering and pain. My pain and my struggle are my own, and I must go through them.

Summer holidays came. Aneeq and Talal were home. My days were full of stress, looking after Raham and trying to protect myself and his brothers from him, and working from home as a hairdresser. Seeing Raham in pain was also heartbreaking for me. He used to have bad headaches and started banging his head against the wall. He even tried to hurt himself by cutting his arm with a knife.

However, things were still difficult. I had to keep an eye on Raham at nighttime so he couldn't escape and hurt himself or his brothers.

Despite all my efforts, Raham managed to escape from home four times. Every time he escaped, it was a big shock for me. He was unwell and vulnerable, and the thought that anything could happen to him shook me to my core. But miraculously, every time he escaped, the police caught him and brought him home safely.

Social workers were coming to visit to check if my kids were safe. One social worker asked Aneeq and Talal if Mum hits them. They both said never, and Talal told them that Raham hits Mum. After a few visits, they closed the case and made the report that the kids are safe.

My friend Iram told me she watched a film on Netflix based on a true story called 'Brain on Fire.' She told me that the girl had the same symptoms as Raham and got the diagnosis that her body was making antibodies, and those antibodies were attacking her brain, causing brain inflammation and behavioural issues. I watched that film and was surprised to see that Raham had the same symptoms. It just clicked for me, and I diagnosed Raham's illness before even doctors did. I knew from the beginning he had brain inflammation, but now I came to know it's antibodies which are causing brain inflammation.

Taking Raham to the appointment was another big task for me. He tried to escape from the car. Sometimes he suddenly attacked me while I was driving to take him to the hospital. I started taking him to the hospital by taxi.

We went to his appointment with a paediatric specialist. The doctor told me that they couldn't find Raham's diagnosis, and it's better if a psychiatrist checks him to find out any possibility of any mental disorder. I told the doctor I could take him to the psychiatrist, but I know my son. There is some physical illness causing his mental health issues. I asked the doctor about antibodies tests. He said they did certain antibodies tests, and they came out negative.

I begged the doctors to repeat all tests again. I had tears in my eyes, and I requested the doctor to do their best to diagnose his illness. The doctor said yes, and he repeated all the tests with some new ones and sent some blood samples to a hospital in London.

Raham had an appointment with a psychiatrist, and while I was taking him for the appointment, I remembered the day when I was taking my mom to a psychiatrist. For a moment, life seemed so unfair. I felt like I came on this earth just to give, not to receive. I felt I came on this earth just to look after others but there is no one to look after me. I started looking after my mom and younger sibling when I was thirteen, and all my life, I've been giving, and now, I was taking care of a sick child who is thirteen. The pain, sadness, and grief took over me. I felt abandoned, like the Universe had abandoned me.

I met Rajni, and she told me that she saw a vision in her meditation about me. She was holding and reading my book, which I wrote, in her vision. I told Rajni about my vision board and putting a picture of a bestseller book, but after that, I never talked or discussed with Rajni about the book as I was more focused on my healing than manifesting goals. I knew deep down when I would be ready, my higher self would help me manifest those dreams, however, in those days when I was at my lowest, thinking about my book and goals were the last thing I could imagine.

When Rajni told me about my book in her vision, I was lost in my suffering, unable to understand what the universe was trying to tell me. The universe wanted me to know that there was a reason for my struggle, that better times would come, and that I would eventually write a book to share my story with others. I didn't fully grasp the meaning of the message, but it offered me a glimmer of hope amid my suffering.

Some people judged me when they saw me in pain. They couldn't understand that despite being spiritual and practising meditation, I could still suffer. One person even asked if I was still meditating. What they failed to realise is that being spiritual or working on personal growth doesn't guarantee a life free of challenges. In fact, it often means confronting our demons, shadows, old wounds, and broken parts of ourselves that we'd rather avoid. Healing is a messy journey filled with ups and downs, and sometimes, facing challenges is necessary for growth.

I continued working from home as much as I could while looking after Raham and my other two kids. There were instances when Raham would come to my workplace at home while I was working and swear and hit me in front of my clients. I felt embarrassed, but thankfully, most of my clients were understanding of the situation.

One afternoon, as I sat analysing why all this was happening to me, I heard my inner voice saying that I was hitting rock bottom. This time, while at rock bottom, I was acutely aware of it, and my mind wandered to how many more rock bottoms I would have to endure.

It had been many months, and Raham's physical and mental illness still hadn't been diagnosed. He was behaving like a toddler, lacking a sense of danger and losing his memory. He couldn't even recognise his best friend from school or Rohan. His violent behaviour towards me was escalating.

I was in pain, shattered, and exhausted. Emotionally, I collapsed. Burnout was setting in, and I found myself losing patience with Raham. One day, amidst his screaming and shouting, I shouted back, telling him to go away and leave me alone. I was angry and contemplated sending him to a care home or even to his father in Pakistan if his mental health didn't improve. The knot in my heart tightened as I longed to escape, even if just for a few days. However, with no family nearby to turn to for a break, I felt trapped.

Episodes of intense anger became frequent. Those who knew me described me as a calm person, but beneath that calmness lay repressed anger poisoning my being. When repressed anger isn't processed healthily, it morphs into rage. During episodes of rage, I retreated to my room, where I cried, screamed, and punched pillows.

Amidst it all, a part of me remained awake and observant. Though at times I lost touch with my conscious awareness and became ensnared in my mind's attempts to shield me from pain, my consciousness always regained control, illuminating my blind spots so I could confront and transform my shadows into light.

As I observed myself, I felt immense shame and guilt for the thoughts I harboured about my ill child and for wanting to escape my struggles and him. Throughout my life, I'd often sought to please others in hopes of gaining their love and attention, crafting an image of myself as a "nice" person. But when my son needed me most, where had that "niceness" vanished? Was I truly a nice girl, or just projecting an image of niceness? That day, stripped of my usual filters, I confronted my raw self and uncovered my selfishness. Despite my facade of selflessness, I realised I'd been wounded, seeking validation from emotionally unavailable people who I believed were better than me. When my vulnerable, ill child needed compassion, where had that good girl gone? I discovered that I was not a good girl when I was merely pleasing others; I was a wounded girl. The wounds within me had opened, revealing the real me, the raw me.

Seeing myself as a screw-up was overwhelming. It was too much to process and too much to heal. I found myself in a total mess, judging and hating myself. Then, the realisation struck that I hadn't fully loved and accepted myself yet I was seeking love from others. How could someone else love and accept me when I couldn't do so for myself? I oscillated between wanting to run away from my son and then berating myself for those thoughts, swinging from one extreme to another.

Feeling broken and lost, I forgot that the universe speaks to us in myriad ways until I opened my phone that day. A video of Dr Shefali popped up, delivering a message of self-love and self-acceptance. She reminded me that self-love isn't just for when things are going right; it's especially vital when we're struggling. Yet, loving and accepting myself in the midst of chaos seemed an insurmountable task.

My mind argued that accepting myself in my mess would mean I wouldn't change, but I realised that wasn't how reality works. It was society's programming, driven by fear and guilt, that coerced us into rejecting our true selves and feelings. Breaking free from societal templates, I chose to accept and love myself as I am. Placing a hand on my heart, I affirmed, "I fully love and accept myself, with compassion for all parts of me."

Fully embracing myself, including my wounds and flaws, was challenging. However, I understood that to have compassion for others, I first needed to show compassion to myself. With self-acceptance came a profound shift within me—confidence, strength, and a newfound compassion that I'd never experienced before.

The knot in my heart wasn't for Raham; it was for me. As I embraced myself fully, that knot loosened. I felt unconditional love for both myself and Raham. I realised I wasn't hating him; I was hating my struggle, resisting the idea of caring for someone with mental health issues due to my own traumas from my mum's struggles.

I began accepting Raham with all his challenges, releasing my expectations and attachments regarding my children's happiness and success. Instead, I recognised that they each had their own soul plans and journeys. My role was to love, protect, respect, and guide them, providing a safe space for them to flourish.

Accepting the inevitability of illness, struggle, pain, and heartbreak for my children might take time, but I knew I was on the right path. One day, I awoke with the knowledge that Raham might not have a long life. Surprisingly, I was okay with that notion, embracing the idea of non-attachment. Yet, I remained unsure of how I'd react when faced with the actuality, uncertain of my subconscious mind's responses, my resistance, and my barriers.

Some people advised me to send Raham to a care home or a teenager care centre. But I decided to take care of Raham, no matter what. My son is seriously ill, and he needs his mum by his side during this difficult time.

As I began to expect the situation and let go of my resistance, clarity started to emerge. I had a sudden realisation about Rajni's behaviour towards me. She had been subtly avoiding me for many months, even before Raham's illness. Despite her emotional unavailability when I needed her most, she was there to offer practical help. Though she asked me a few times if I needed assistance, she was emotionally distant and neglectful in subtle ways that I initially failed to notice.

Over time, I began to observe, notice, and gain clarity on how long she had been ignoring me. While I regularly invited her to my house, she hadn't invited me to hers in months, despite living just a two-minute drive away. For months, it felt like our friendship was one-sided, with me putting in more effort. As I processed her strange behaviour, I found myself withdrawing from her. It was heartbreaking to consider that my best friend was ignoring me, someone I trusted deeply.

As I distanced myself, Rajni noticed the change. She assumed my reduced communication was due to depression or distress, prompting her to send a mutual friend to check on me. Although well-intentioned, I didn't divulge details about Rajni, as we never spoke ill of each other to others.

After much reflection, I surmised that Rajni's neglect might stem from her family attachments. Being family-oriented and in an unhealthy relationship, she may have felt threatened by my single motherhood and pursuit of personal freedom and empowerment.

A few days later, Rajni visited me, expressing concern over my behaviour. I explained that I wasn't depressed, but rather, her actions were affecting me. I confronted her about not treating me like family, not inviting me over, and only making time for me when convenient for her.

Before I could finish, Rajni became defensive, blaming me instead of listening. Despite this being only the second time I'd raised a genuine concern, she seemed unwilling to hear me out. Her defensiveness stemmed from feeling attacked and inadequate in our friendship.

When she expressed feeling inferior, I was taken aback, unable to believe what I was hearing. As Rajni spoke, her pain became apparent, stripped of any facade or filter. Witnessing her vulnerability, I realised that her ego was attempting to shield her from her insecurities, but I saw beyond that, witnessing her true self.

Her eyes were down, preventing her from seeing my surprised expression. I told her if you always feel small in front of me, why didn't you discuss it with me before? She couldn't respond to that. I assured her that I never intended to make her feel small and suggested she might have self-esteem issues to address. However, she dismissed this completely, denying any such issues.

Her defensiveness made it difficult for me to express myself fully, and my codependent, apologetic tendencies took over as I didn't want to risk losing her. As she left, I found myself apologising, saying I didn't mean to hurt her. She accepted the apology, and that was that.

I always treated Rajni as a special person in my life, boosting her self-esteem and supporting her healing journey. I was always proud of her psychic gifts, and more than I could confess at that time, her companionship was indeed a guiding light to me. Her accusation that I made her feel small hurt me deeply. I couldn't fathom in what way had I made my friend feel this way? Going back to a million conversations in my mind, I tried to find any speck of insult I may have hurled her way, but I couldn't find any. I cried for hours after she left.

The next day, she texted me, expressing a desire to maintain our friendship and inviting me to brunch at her house to make amends.

Attending her brunch, I sensed a different energy between us, a tension that hadn't been there before. It felt as though she was trying to please me, not from the heart, but to salvage our friendship. Despite this, I went because I didn't want to lose what we had.

As I continued to process our conflict, I received a message from the hospital informing me of Raham's appointment with a Rheumatologist.

Accompanying Raham to the appointment, we learned he was diagnosed with cerebral lupus, with certain antibodies attacking his brain and body. The doctor explained that lupus is a lifelong illness, treated with chemotherapy among other methods. Hearing this news saddened me deeply, despite my prior understanding that Raham might never fully recover.

Returning home with a heavy heart, I had no one to share Raham's diagnosis with. I didn't feel comfortable discussing it with Rajni, given the strained state of our relationship.

Reflecting on Rajni's behaviour, I concluded that she was trapped in her ego, experiencing her own dark night of the soul. While I suspected she had self-esteem issues, she denied it, leaving me unsure how to proceed. It became clear to me that she needed a significant inner transformation, but I realised it wasn't my responsibility to initiate that change. She had made it clear that she didn't want me to pressure her into personal growth.

I realised Rajni needed a significant inner transformation before we could rebuild our friendship, and it wasn't my responsibility to change her, especially since she denied having self-esteem issues. She made it clear that she didn't want me to push her towards personal growth, saying it stressed her out. This left me with no option to discuss what was happening between us, as she feared feeling small in front of me again.

My codependent tendencies urged me to ignore what she said, to make myself small to please her, or to sweep everything under the rug to salvage our friendship. But I chose to listen to my higher self, acknowledging the need to be true, authentic, and honest with myself. If I couldn't be honest with myself, I couldn't be honest with her or anyone else. So, I made the difficult decision to let her go from my life.

Throughout my life, I hadn't been honest with myself, often saying yes when I meant no, and vice versa. It was time to stand for my truth and be prepared to let go of anyone in my life by speaking that truth.

I stopped communicating with Rajni. It was the first time in our years of friendship that I ignored her messages and calls. On a hot summer day, as she persistently called and messaged me, I finally texted her, expressing my decision not to continue our friendship. It was a heart-wrenching moment, feeling like my world was crumbling as I let go of someone so dear to me.

My higher self reassured me that even if I were alone, I would be fine. I needed to accept my aloneness, recognising that I came into this world alone and would leave it alone. It was time to release my dependency on others and embrace my personal power, even though it wasn't easy.

During a walk in the park, tears streaming down my cheeks, I found solace in each step towards my personal power, shedding attachments and expectations along the way. The walk became a meditation, catalysing a significant transformation within me. As I reached the end of my walk, I encountered Rajni waiting for me at the car park.

She explained that she had taken time off work as I hadn't been responding to her calls and messages, expressing a desire to talk. I explained that I had attempted difficult conversations with her previously to no avail, and if we couldn't have those discussions, I preferred not to engage at all. Despite her lingering ego, I detected cracks this time.

Expressing my hurt and anger, I confronted her about her words and behaviour, questioning how I could make her feel small while always treating her as special in my life. Though she attempted excuses, I made it clear they wouldn't suffice. She had no response, finally understanding the impact of her actions and words.

I told her, "It's not just about me; you've been stuck for so many months, and I can only help you if you want to help yourself." She expressed readiness to accept my help, and we decided to meet at my house in a few days to discuss the deeper issues she was facing. I emphasised the importance of coming with an open heart and mind.

When she arrived at my house, I was surprised to see that she hadn't brought her ego with her. I noticed it seemed shattered, as she had surrendered it for the sake of our friendship. Rajni's willingness to let go of her ego for our friendship was something I couldn't forget, and I remain grateful for her courage in doing so. She realised she had two options: to choose her ego or to choose me, and she chose me.

Seeing me be honest with myself, speaking my truth, and standing strong in my authenticity gave her the courage to connect with her authentic self. Despite being stuck in the dark night of the soul phase for over a year, Rajni never stopped her daily meditation and spiritual practices, which helped her connect with her higher self.

I advised Rajni to process her pain and work on her self-esteem by affirming, "I am enough." I suggested she try inner child meditation, which I found helpful at the beginning of my spiritual awakening. During our long conversation, I illuminated her blind spots so she could work on them. She listened to me with an open heart and mind, showing no resistance.

Rajni practised inner child meditation, allowing herself to sit with her pain and process it while working on her self-esteem. In the following days, she texted me, expressing that she had been holding onto too much pain but had finally let it out and processed it. She admitted feeling lost but thanked me for being a ray of light in her life and helping her see her blind spots.

Our friendship underwent a major transformation, and we felt a significant shift in our energy and consciousness. Our connection and trust in each other deepened. Even before Raham's condition improved, I found myself getting better. Through my inner transformation, I became emotionally mature, strong, and resilient. The pain, resistance, and numbness I had carried for six months dissipated as I faced my demons, felt all the dense emotions, and witnessed my weaknesses and emotional immaturity.

Despite moments when my mind told me it was too much to handle, I found the courage to persevere through the storm. Emerging from that storm, I felt like a new person. The dark tunnel I had felt trapped in was a construct of my mind and shadows. In reality, I had always been loved and guided by my source. The lessons I learned in those six months of challenges would have taken me a lifetime to learn.

Raham's treatment for lupus began with chemotherapy alongside immunosuppressants and steroids. When Raham learned about chemotherapy, he was scared of losing his hair and being bald. The nurse reassured us that ten percent of people don't lose their hair during chemotherapy.

Raham's first few treatments were challenging. It was difficult to take him to the hospital. I used to accompany him in Rajni's car to keep an eye on him so he wouldn't run away. In the hospital, he would shout and break things. He was still angry with me because of his treatment and would throw things. However, after a few weeks, the treatment began to take effect, and he started to improve. Fortunately, he didn't lose his hair, and the hair he had lost due to lupus grew back.

Chapter 8 – A Journey Unveiled

Seven Bodies

Rajni told me she felt she had another awakening and self-realisation, that "she knows nothing." I had a similar realisation during my second awakening. I also felt like I had another awakening. Although I had researched different stages of spiritual awakening and levels of consciousness, that information did not resonate with me.

Does awakening happen in episodes? Seeking answers, I started reading Osho's book "In Search of the Miraculous," which discusses chakras, kundalini, and the seven bodies. According to Osho, we are not just a physical body; there are seven bodies, each corresponding to a chakra. Each chakra is intricately connected to its corresponding body. "Within them lie all the means as well as barriers. Therefore, there is not much reason to inquire outside."

"The first chakra of the physical body is the root chakra. This chakra has an integral connection with the physical body. The root chakra has two possibilities. Its first potentiality is natural and given to us at birth; its other possibility is obtainable through meditation."

In the first awakening, we activate our root chakra, healing any energetic blockages in our first body, and transcend it.

The second body is called the etheric body, which is connected to the second chakra. The second body is the emotional body. Transformation happens in the emotional body when the meditator transcends hate, anger, fear, and violence into love, compassion, fearlessness, and friendliness.

The third body is the astral body, which is connected to the third chakra. According to the book, "primarily the third body revolves around doubt and thinking. If these are transformed, doubt becomes trust, and thinking becomes Vivek (awareness)."

The fourth body is the mental body, which is connected to the fourth chakra. As Osho says, a person whose fourth body faculties are functioning has great psychic abilities, such as telepathy, clairvoyance, thought projection, and thought reading, to see the truth, to see the real. According to Osho, a person on the fourth plane is ready to receive grace (divine energy).

The fifth body is the spiritual body, which is connected to the throat chakra. According to Osho, one who has entered the fifth body is completely rid of all unconsciousness. Such a person is forever awake, even in sleep. A person in the fifth body can be called a "Buddha" (an awakened one). Suffering ends in the fifth body, and the person feels ecstasy, joy, and bliss.

The sixth body is the cosmic body, which is connected to the third eye chakra. According to Osho, mysticism starts on the sixth plane. In the sixth body, one can witness the vast infinite expanse that the third eye reveals. They can now view the cosmic and the infinite.

The seventh plane is Nirvana, which is connected to the seventh chakra, the crown chakra. Nirvana is ultimate enlightenment when someone transcends everything and becomes one with the source.

After reading that book, I realised I had entered the third "astral" body, which is why I felt a third awakening. Rajni entered the second "etheric" body with her second awakening.

Humans have a tendency to get comfortable even in uncomfortable situations. When we experience spiritual awakening and start feeling the connection with our soul and the source, as well as begin to see the beauty of life, there is a greater chance that we can become stuck on any particular plane. Therefore, struggles, challenges, and shocks are needed to go deep within so that we don't remain stuck at the surface level of joy and peace. Challenges and triggers help us identify and heal our deep blockages and wounds, enabling us to move from one plane of awakening to another.

The challenges Rajni and I faced helped us progress to the next body. In my case, the amount of struggle and suffering I endured allowed me to overcome my fear and resistance to struggle and suffering. I told Rajni that I am no longer afraid of the challenges and suffering in life.

When transitioning from one body to another, there was a transition period that lasted a few weeks. During this time, Rajni and I were extremely open to new information and spiritual insights. We watched videos and read books religiously. By October 2022, we had settled into our new plane.

Moving into the next body was a significant upgrade of energy, and Rajni and I felt like we were on cloud nine again. We were having a great time, feeling happy and cheerful. We started seeing each other regularly, going for walks, having coffee, and shopping more often.

Raham was improving with treatment, and his memory started to return. He never fully recovered mentally, and lupus still affects his physical and mental health. However, after treatment, he never became violent with me or tried to escape from the house again.

After entering the third plane, I had one episode of repressed anger. The kids did something that triggered this anger. I felt the intense energy of rage emerging, but because I was consciously aware of my emotions, I started observing myself and the changes in my body and breathing as I processed and transcended my rage. I might have looked funny to my kids, and they started laughing at me. Then I started smiling because I intuitively knew this was my last episode of rage. I had faced and processed one of my demons: repressed anger.

Repressed anger occurs when we live in unhealthy and toxic environments and do not have space to express our anger healthily. When we control and suppress our anger, the energy of that anger goes deep into our system and becomes rage. This rage can be triggered by small things that wouldn't normally make us angry in our natural state.

I still have healthy anger, which is a normal emotion given by existence to protect ourselves. The anger Rajni saw as a demon in her meditation was repressed anger, which we need to transcend to heal ourselves and raise our vibrations.

The Lost Friend

Rohan called me after three months. I was sure I had blocked his number, but somehow it became unblocked mysteriously, and he managed to ring me. Perhaps we still had lessons to learn from each other.

He didn't ask me how I had been managing my challenges or how I was taking care of Raham. I told him that Raham had been diagnosed with cerebral lupus, but he didn't pay much attention and started talking as if nothing had happened. He mentioned that he was talking to a girl in Pakistan and wanted to marry her and bring her to the UK.

After witnessing his behaviour during his infatuation and how he turned his back on me during my difficult times, I adjusted my expectations of him. I welcomed him back into my life with a new perspective.

He told me that no man would want to be in a relationship with me or marry me because I am a mother of three children. He suggested that I would only be able to marry when my children were grown and independent. However, I didn't accept his view because I was beginning to understand my self-worth.

The reason for his statement was that he noticed how emotionally close I was with my children and that they were my priority. He believed that I would never ignore my kids for any man, whether a friend or a partner. He thought I would never be able to love and give time to a partner because I was busy with my kids. He could not see that a good mother, who is sincere with her children, would also be a loyal and sincere partner. A man with awareness would see these qualities as positive attributes, not as red flags.

Another reason he said that was because of his upbringing in Pakistan. In Eastern cultures, there is a belief that a woman's desirability for marriage or as a romantic partner diminishes if she has children or is divorced. I was twice divorced, a busy mum with three kids, and had one ill child. He didn't want to marry a woman with children because he had no place in his heart or mind to care for someone else's kids. He thought that if he couldn't do it, no other man could. He didn't realise he was speaking from his own programming and societal beliefs. I believe that a man with an open, loving heart and mind can not only love and accept me for who I am but also accept my children wholeheartedly. Until I find that man, I will wait and never lose hope in love.

Rohan didn't have a deep understanding of narcissism, nor had he done his own research on the topic. He told me that his mum was a narcissist. When his mum came to visit from Pakistan, he brought her to my house. I invited Rajni as well, so she could meet his mum and keep her company.

Rajni and I really liked Rohan's mum. She was warm and caring, and we had a good time with her. I found out she was not a narcissist. She gave me her number, and we started talking occasionally. She had raised her children as a single mother and understood my struggles as a single mum with an ill child. She showed a lot of compassion for Raham and frequently checked on his well-being.

I told Rohan that his mum was not a narcissist. I realised he had brought her to my house and mentioned me proudly to his friends and family, not because he was genuinely proud of me, but to inflate his ego. He had extremely low self-esteem and a lack of self-worth. My friendship boosted his ego, showing the world that someone cared about him, which made him feel like he mattered.

When he returned, he called me regularly and behaved normally for the first few weeks, but then he started behaving coldly again. This time, he was very careful. He never ignored my messages or calls because he knew I wouldn't tolerate it and he could lose my friendship. However, when he spoke to me on the phone, there was no warmth in his voice, unlike before.

He was planning to marry the girl he had been talking to and was infatuated with her. Once his infatuation phase ended, he got bored and stopped talking to her. She was hurt by his behaviour, having dreamt of a future with him, and sent him long, sad text messages expressing her heartbreak.

I realised he was addicted to infatuation. When someone becomes addicted to their own hormones to feel high and distract themselves from their pain and misery, they can quickly lose interest once the hormonal rush subsides. He would treat the girl like a queen, making her feel like his world revolved around her. But once his infatuation ended and his hormones returned to normal, he felt so low, drained, and lost that he didn't want to see her face or even hear her voice.

What he did to me, he also did to that girl, and he had done it to many girls before me. I witnessed his infatuation four times, including with me, in the span of one year. He was unaware of his unhealthy pattern, as all addictions result from unconscious behaviour. I made him aware of how his unhealthy behaviour was hurting other women, although I didn't use the word "addiction" as it could have been too much for him to handle with his low self-esteem. Although he never paid attention when I talked about healing and spirituality, he realised that he was doing something terrible to women. The text messages from the last girl also made him feel guilty, and he decided not to repeat that pattern. But he didn't know that you cannot stop an addiction or unhealthy behaviour through mental effort alone. There is always a reason within us, and to overcome addiction or any unhealthy behaviour, we need to look within ourselves, find, understand, and heal the wound that is causing the pattern. Rohan lacked the courage to go within and face his demons. He kept running from his healing and continued to get lost in darkness.

He stopped love bombing girls to trigger his feelings and hormones, but he continued talking to many girls in Pakistan to find a match, although now he was very careful.

My Deep Blind Spots

After entering the third plane of spirituality, I began to have awareness of my deep wounds and blind spots that I was carrying in my third body, which were shaping my personality. That codependent personality, and unhealthy beliefs and ideas which I borrowed from societal programming and used as coping mechanisms to survive abuse.

Osho said, "Unless you drop your personality, you will not be able to find your individuality." It was time for me to let go of my personality, connect to my soul's essence, and find my individuality.

I realised that I was attached to romantic love and it was time to let go of that attachment. I was able to see those deep attachments with my inner eyes and conscious awareness. Because I didn't receive love growing up as a child, I believed that romantic love would fulfil all my emotional needs that were never met and fill the emptiness I was carrying within me. Because of these beliefs, I used to fantasise about romantic love and had unrealistic expectations from my romantic partners. These very attachments were becoming barriers to attracting love into my life.

For two days, I witnessed these attachments. Then I let them go by recognising, acknowledging, accepting, and diving deep into why they were there. I felt a shift in myself because I transformed the energy of these attachments into joy and love.

The Over-Giver

After one month, I received another insight that I was an over-giver and had a saviour complex. I had an idea that I had been giving too much all my life, but this insight was so loud and clear that it made me fully aware of my over-giving nature. It was like shedding the light of my conscious awareness on my blind spots, which I had been unaware of, and because of this unawareness, I was living in the darkness of my own deep shadows.

I became aware of why I was over-giving and trying to save other people. I was over-giving due to an inner lack of self-worth and self-love. I learned as a child growing up in an abusive environment that love needed to be earned by giving too much and putting in too much effort. I was over-giving to get others' attention, love, and validation. I was over-giving to feel superior, powerful, competent, and in control.

Because of my over-giving, I was attracting broken and narcissistic people into my life and kept repeating the cycle. By over-giving, I was taking on the responsibility of others, leading to burnout and feeling overwhelmed.

It took me a few days to energetically transform my over-giver and saviour shadows, but it took many more months to reset my over-giver mindset and create new neurological pathways in my brain. Our minds take more time to change physically than to heal energetically.

I realised that I was trying to rescue Rohan due to my saviour complex, which was now using my spirituality in a sneaky way to save others. I was over-giving in my friendships. I let go of my urge to save Rohan as I realised it is not my job to change or rescue others. Unconditional love means accepting a person for who they are, not who we wish them to be. When the universe respects our free will, who am I to try to force someone to heal?

When I let go of my efforts to rescue Rohan, I noticed he was enjoying the attention I was giving him by trying to heal him, yet at the same time, he was resisting healing and any kind of personal growth. I started giving less, but my love and care for him did not diminish. I was giving and behaving in a healthier way.

The Struggle Mindset

Raham's treatment finished, and he went to school for a few days but then stopped because of his joint pains and other health issues caused by lupus. One part of me was still struggling because of his illness.

In January 2023, I received an insight that I have a struggle mindset. I believed that life is a struggle, a belief rooted in my childhood when I struggled to survive in an abusive and chaotic environment. Knowing that I had a struggle mindset was an eye-opening moment for me. I wondered if I was manifesting struggle in my life because of this mindset. Perhaps I was.

After realising this, I commanded my mind to believe that life is not a struggle. As I read in "Conversations with God," "You are here to celebrate life." Life is a gift from God, and the truth is that life is easy, simple, and beautiful. It is our mind and ego that make life complicated.

Rajni was getting better at receiving messages in her meditation. Initially, she received messages that the universe wanted us to know. Then she started asking questions and receiving answers.

I requested Rajni to ask about Raham as I felt there was more to come. I told Rajni I was okay with knowing anything because I am not afraid of anything now. Rajni asked the question before meditating and saw a vision of Raham sitting in a wheelchair. She was also told that Raham's condition would help me to surrender.

I was okay hearing that, but after knowing it, I stopped worrying about Raham's education. I became more relaxed and let him do whatever made him happy. Raham's illness and Rajni's vision helped me learn not to worry about the future and to live in the present moment.

I did not want my other two children to suffer because of Raham's illness, as I knew from experience how childhood struggles and trauma affect our future lives. My other children were happy and doing well in school. However, they did occasionally get frustrated with Raham's behaviour, but they still loved him, cared about him, and even helped by giving him water and passing things to him.

Despite Raham's health issues and numerous hospital appointments, I was living a normal and happy life. My personal growth and ascension were accelerating, and I was growing rapidly as a person day by day.

I decided to start my search for the love of my life again, so I began going on dates. I talked to many men and went on several dates, but I found that most of them were wounded and lost. One man I went on a few dates with turned out to be a narcissist. As soon as I realised this, I told him we were not compatible and blocked his number. I was shocked to discover that I was still attracting narcissists.

It had been more than five years since I had been single, and I was still struggling to find the love of my life. I felt a little disappointed, but then I remembered a spiritual woman who had come to my salon and given me a message that the universe would send me a man who would love me. Now I understood why the universe sent that woman with a message—because I had to go through so much struggle to find love, that message gave me hope, and I never stopped believing in love, no matter how many failed dates I had and how many narcissists I attracted.

Unable to See Negativity

As I was going about my days, I found myself asking the universe why I was still attracting narcissistic people into my life. I had an insight into another blind spot: I was too positive. I focused only on the good in people, and my mind could not show me negativity. This was a trauma response from my childhood, designed to protect me from pain. Because there was so much pain, my brain adapted certain functions as coping mechanisms to save me. It served me well and helped me survive as a child in a painful, abusive environment.

Around that time, I came across a video in which a psychiatrist explained that children growing up in abusive environments often have an underactive left frontal cortex, hampering their ability to reason and pay attention to all aspects of reality, both negative and positive. The right frontal cortex, on the other hand, becomes overactive, flooding them with emotions and suppressing reasoning, thus creating an inability to see reality as it is.

That information resonated with me. During all this, I met a man who used love bombing to ensnare me on our dates, giving me all his attention and praise, which triggered my emotions. There were many red flags, but because I was overwhelmed with emotions and unable to reason and see the negativity, my brain filtered out those red flags. After a month of seeing each other, when he thought he had me under his control, he started showing his narcissistic traits. Because I was aware of narcissism, I spotted it as soon as it appeared.

Once I became aware of my blind spot, I commanded my brain to show me reality as it is, including the negativity, as I am now an adult, mature enough to see and handle it.

It wasn't that I was entirely unable to see negativity, but my mind was filtering reality and not showing me all the negativity as it was. Meditation and spiritual awakening also bring light codes to the brain, activating the dim parts so that the brain starts working more efficiently. During my spiritual awakening, I was experiencing major energy upgrades and ascension.

Although since my awakening I had become more aware of my blind spots and those of people around me, when I started activating the dim and inactive parts of my brain, I began seeing reality more clearly, including the negativity. And there was a lot of negativity and darkness around me.

Letting Go of Negativity with Love

As I became a healthier version of myself, a few people around me, including Rohan, began behaving in more unhealthy ways. I knew there was a spiritual reason for our friendship, and I always cared for, respected, and loved him.

In his mind, he entered my life to find a distraction from his misery. However, because of my care, respect, and love for him, he didn't realise that he was starting to get attached to me.

I began noticing his attachments to me. When I started talking to other men to find love, he didn't like it. When I used to tell him about my dates, he never paid attention. Once, I asked him if he was jealous, and he responded with agitation in our Urdu language, which means "jealous, my shoes." He didn't realise that even as he said this, he exuded a jealous energy which I could see and feel.

For my fortieth birthday in 2023, I decided to throw a big party. At that time, I was talking to a new guy and was very happy and excited. When Rohan came to my birthday party, both Rajni and I noticed that he seemed lost, confused, and depressed.

I started seeing my friend Iram more often because I felt she needed help with her healing and spirituality, as she wasn't meditating regularly. I gave her a few books, and she started reading them and meditating irregularly. She told me that every morning around half past four, she felt as though someone nonphysical was waking her up to remind her to meditate, but she still wasn't listening. She had visions during meditation for her healing, but she continued to resist her calling for awakening.

As I saw her regularly, Rohan, Rajni, and I became mutual friends. I had the feeling that if Rohan and Iram could heal themselves, they could make a good couple. I told Rohan that if he healed himself, I could find him a good partner. He understood what I was implying and began flirting with Iram rather than focusing on his healing. Iram gave the impression that she wasn't interested in marriage or a relationship, but as soon as Rohan started flirting with her, she began enjoying his attention. I wasn't expecting this; I knew they were both not ready for a healthy relationship yet. However, because they were adults and responsible for their actions, I didn't take it seriously. In fact, I was amused to see how happy Iram was to receive Rohan's attention, even though it was just a little.

Rohan's mum and brother came from Pakistan, and I invited them to my house. I also invited Iram and Rajni, but Rajni couldn't come because she was busy. After tea at my house, I took them to the park where Iram joined us. I had never seen Iram so happy before. Rohan, however, was still lost in his misery and did not seem happy.

He was thinking that I had rejected him as a partner because he felt he wasn't good enough, and he was experiencing immense pain from this perceived rejection. For a moment, as an empath, I experienced his pain in my body and read his mind. I was surprised to learn this, as I had accepted him as my best friend while he thought I had rejected him as a romantic partner. I realised this stemmed from his low self-esteem and lack of self-worth.

After the park, Iram went home, and I took Rohan's mum and brother out for dinner because I wanted to treat them. I had a good time with his mum, whom I found very sweet. When I came home after dinner, Iram called me. She was still happy and told me a few things that made me realise she was imagining marrying Rohan.

Rohan was not serious about her; he was just flirting with her, and he wanted to get married in Pakistan. Iram knew that he was talking to girls in Pakistan and that he wasn't talking to her regularly. Still, she was dreaming and fantasising about marrying him because of her delusion that he loved her.

Rohan was extremely confused in his life. It seemed like he didn't have one mind; he was torn between many conflicting thoughts. One part of him wanted one thing, while another part wanted the opposite. I nicknamed him "confuse.com" because of his confused and lost mind.

One day, Rohan rang me and told me about a vivid dream he had. In his dream, he saw the love of his life, a spiritual woman. He said she wasn't me. She was sitting in meditation, her face obscured, and she was telling him to repeat a few affirmations: "I am enough. I love myself. I am open to receiving good things in my life."

I already knew he needed to work on his self-esteem. I was amazed by how loved and supported we are by our creator. Rohan wasn't listening to me or his calling for healing. The universe knew that romantic love was his weakness, so it tried to help him through his love of life, respecting his free will. But again, he did not do any of those affirmations even once.

At the beginning of our friendship, Iram never asked for help. As soon as I started helping her and we became close, her expectations grew more and more, seemingly without end. She began trying to control and manipulate me to get what she wanted. She became angry if I said no to something. She even tried to make me feel bad by criticising my body and my house cleaning. She also became clingy and wanted to go almost everywhere with me.

She confused my ego-lessness, kindness, openness, adaptability, and lack of a guard, which I had achieved through much healing and work, for weakness. She dropped her masks, not realising that although I had no ego and carried no guard, I had consciousness and, with my conscious awareness, sense of self-worth, and self-love, I could protect myself.

As her mask dropped, I saw her raw self without any filter, just as I had seen mine and Rajni's. Since I saw myself without any filter and was able to see my blind spots, I was becoming better at seeing others without filters and their blind spots.

I saw that behind her arrogance were low self-esteem, self-hatred, and a negative self-image. I witnessed her wrong beliefs, huge ego, unhealthy mindset, wounds, and blind spots that extended deep into her being. She was trying to project her pain onto me, not understanding where I was coming from. People who don't know themselves cannot know others. Unconsciously, she was expecting me to behave codependently, but my codependency was on its last breath.

She couldn't see the positivity in me or others, just as I couldn't see negativity in others. Because she couldn't see, she couldn't appreciate my efforts and kindness towards her.

She had deep attachments to money, and because of this, she tried to exploit me financially. I was surprised to find that she wasn't honest in money matters. Rajni and I are always honest about money; we consider each other's losses as our own and never have issues related to money. But Iram wasn't like us.

She behaved narcissistically towards me, like a two-year-old stubborn child throwing tantrums. She was also not a good receiver and resisted my kind, compassionate, and helpful behaviour towards her. At the same time, her ego enjoyed the special treatment I had been giving her for the past few months.

I realised that whatever good and kind treatment I was giving her, it was inflating her ego. I decided not to entertain her ego anymore, as I am not here to feed someone's ego, especially when I don't even feed my own.

I tried to talk to her on the phone. I simply told her to relax and focus on her meditation. She became not just defensive but also tried to wind me up mentally. I ended the call, saying goodbye. She immediately sent me a long text message with complaints. I noticed her compulsive behaviour and decided to create some space from her.

I stopped talking to her as I processed all her unreasonable behaviour. I saw narcissism in her, but I am not the kind of person who labels someone a narcissist easily unless I confirm it intuitively. Over time, I started trusting my intuition more, and I waited to know intuitively if she was a narcissist. A few days later, I woke up with the realisation that she was indeed a narcissist. Even though I had seen her narcissistic behaviour over the past few weeks, I was still surprised. I texted Rajni to tell her about my intuition. She was also surprised and asked if I was sure it wasn't just my mind. I told her I trust my intuition and it wasn't my mind.

As soon as I found out she was a narcissist, I decided to end the friendship and blocked her number. I wasn't sad, angry, or heartbroken as I had no attachments or expectations from her.

I do not believe in dehumanising narcissistic people. I believe they are wounded individuals who can heal themselves if they want to. Iram had her calling for awakening, and if her ego ever surrendered, she could start listening to her higher self and choose the right path, which could lead her to healing and light. I blocked Iram because I needed to protect myself and not let myself be used and abused by her narcissism and ego.

After blocking her, she didn't text Rajni or any of my friends, but she kept texting Rohan. I didn't play the victim or feel sad. I told Rohan that she was trying to use me, and when I realised she was a narcissist, I blocked her. Rohan asked if he could do something to patch things up with her, and I told him to stay away from the matter, but he didn't listen to me.

I noticed he tried to take her side in a very subtle way. I knew one of the reasons he was siding with Iram was his belief that it is not good to leave a friendship or relationship. He believed that people who leave are horrible because his dad left when he was just five years old. The sudden abandonment by his dad and the struggle that followed left a huge impact on his psyche. He was still not mature enough to understand that sometimes leaving someone can be the most loving thing you can do for both the other person and yourself. If a friendship or relationship isn't working, leaving can prevent further suffering and psychological damage.

I was planning to take the kids on holiday in the summer. I was not comfortable taking Raham alone because of his health and mental health issues. He had anxiety, joint pain, and was on anti-anxiety medicine. I asked Rohan if he could join us if I paid for him as well. He agreed. After booking the holiday, Rohan jokingly said, "What if something happens between us on holiday?" I told him not to say that ever again and that it would never happen because I trust myself and I trust him as well.

One of the reasons he was still romantically fantasising about me was that he realised I am open-minded and do not behave in a certain way like other Pakistani women due to their conditioning. I do not have body shame, I look after my body, I feel confident, and I wear Western clothes. In our Pakistani society, there is a certain mindset that if a woman wears certain clothes, looks after herself, is bold and not shy, and represents herself well, if she is divorced and single, she is seen as a loose woman doing it to get men's attention.

It wasn't just Rohan; many men in our community, even married men, approached me in real life and through social media, thinking I was representing myself to get men's attention. These types of men do not know that a confident and strong woman who can protect herself is a high-value woman who knows her self-worth. She respects her body, loves herself, and looks after herself for her own sake, not for others.

We went on holiday, and Rohan was behaving well with the kids, but he was indifferent towards me and emanating negative energy. I witnessed resentment in him towards me. He told me that he was talking to Iram and had sent her pictures of our holiday. Iram sent him a message while we were away, which he showed me. I was okay with that and didn't mind him talking to her. I knew Iram sent him the message thinking I would be jealous, and Rohan showed it to me to make me feel bad.

For the first few days, I was okay, but on the last day of our holiday, I absorbed his increasingly intense negative energy. Despite this, I continued to see him through my positive projection and justified his behaviour in my mind, thinking he was good with my kids, especially since Raham had a good time with him.

When we returned from the holiday and he was going home, I noticed a sense of resentment and disgust in his energy towards me. Although he said nothing, his body language and energy made me very uncomfortable. I kept ignoring his strange behaviour towards me as I still held his positive image in my mind, which he had created at the beginning of our friendship by showing his niceness.

Raham started having a flare-up of lupus, but this time it was not serious, and the doctor recommended a few treatments again. Raham was still very resistant to treatment and refused to receive it every time we went to the hospital. He locked himself in the toilet and broke the wires of the IV treatment. I told Rohan about Raham's treatment, but he never asked me about his health, treatment, or my struggles with him.

I mentioned to Rohan that he doesn't ask about Raham and is still unable to see my struggle with Raham. I told him that just because I don't complain or mourn, it doesn't mean I am not struggling with my son's serious illness. A good friend should care about what another friend is going through.

Rohan again did not understand what I meant. He asked me once how Raham was doing, but I could feel he was just asking out of formality.

Raham's illness kept me grounded; otherwise, there was a good chance I would feel high and might not be able to see and work on my deep blind spots. To the world, I was living a good life. I was happy, cheerful, and enjoying my life, yet one part of me was still struggling because of Raham's illness.

Transcending My Receiving Block

Since I noticed a few of my deep blind spots, I was interested in discovering more, as I have always been curious. So, I came up with one mantra: "Dear God, my spirit guides and angels, show me my blind spot."

I said that mantra after my meditation, and in the next few days, I had an insight that I was blocked from receiving love and financial support from men. I felt a huge energetic block around me, which was preventing me from receiving from men.

I was not expecting to see what I had been shown. I was surprised to know that, and it was so deep that my mind initially resisted accepting it. My mind was trying to protect me from the pain of realising that it was me, and because of my block, I was attracting men into my life who were unable to love me and provide financially. Flashes of memories came to my mind of how my two husbands wanted me to work and provide for them financially.

Because I was blocked from receiving, I was attracting men who were blocked from giving. If I had a block for receiving, they had a block for giving. That's why we clicked, alongside other reasons.

After a week of diving deep into my receiving block, I transcended it by recognising, accepting, and acknowledging it. I felt an openness to receive and a major shift of energy within me. Since I was able to see my own block for receiving, I gained the ability to see receiving and giving blocks in others.

The Deep Desire of Men's Love

The more I got to know myself, the more I wanted to know. As soon as I transcended my receiving block, I asked again: "Dear God, my spirit guides and angels, show me my blind spots." In the next few days, I had the insight that I have a deep desire for romantic love. Because of this deep desire, I craved romantic love.

I was again surprised to discover this, as after healing my attachments to love, I thought I had healed my love blocks and was ready to manifest love. However, there was still a huge block that needed to be cleared to manifest romantic love. For one week, I dived deep into my love block. I saw the energetic block with my inner eye and the craving for love in the depth of my being. That block was not just in my mind; it was in every cell of my being. The more I focused on it, the more I witnessed it.

There is a Buddha quote: "Desire is the root cause of suffering." First, I was blocked from receiving love, then I had a deep desire to be loved. Desire comes from wanting something, and "I want" means "I don't have." If I have "I don't have" energy in my system, it means lack, and I cannot attract love while believing in a lack of love. The deep desire and craving repels love energy instead of attracting and keeping love.

I knew that my true nature and soul energy is love, and I must let go of the desire and craving for love. Then I will vibrate at my true frequency, which is nothing but love, and from that true vibration of love, by being love, I will be able to attract love into my life. I dived deep into my desire and craving for man's love, and after one week, that desire and craving energy transcended into love energy.

After healing that, I no longer craved love from someone or wanted someone to complete me, as I felt whole and complete within myself. However, I still have a healthy desire to experience and share romantic love, and I know intuitively that my soul also wants to experience a healthy romantic partnership in this lifetime.

I learned from my experience that there is a difference between healthy desire and unhealthy desire. Unhealthy desires are when we want something desperately, with attachments from our past wounds, and believing in lack. These very desires become blocks to manifesting our intentions into reality. Healthy desires are intentions to manifest something that is in alignment with your soul's purpose in this lifetime, without any attachment to the outcome, by having faith in the universe and knowing that you are already love and abundant.

In August 2023, I was working on my deep blind spots while taking Raham to appointments for treatment every two weeks. Rohan came to my house because my kids wanted his help to buy a PlayStation. He was talking to a girl in Pakistan and planning to get married. He had stopped having long talks with me, but that day he sat with me in the back garden and started talking about Iram. He said many things which made me realise he was talking to her regularly and took her side when I blocked her. He told me Iram was speaking negatively about me and said that he felt negative about me because of it. After talking about Iram, at the end of the conversation, he said, "I know if I have a difficult time, you will be there to help me."

Two egos temporarily united to dim my light. He said many things that he had previously hidden from me to avoid losing my friendship by taking Iram's side. I knew he was talking to Iram, and I did not care about that, as I believe in personal freedom. As long as he was loyal to me, I did not care who he was talking to. However, he was hiding things from me, and when he noticed I did not care at all, he told me everything, even exaggerating to make me feel bad, as his desperation to dim my light grew.

I was busy with my healing and Raham's recent flare-up of lupus and treatment. I was not even slightly concerned if Rohan was talking to Iram or not, but the truth fell into my lap.

When he called me in the next few days, I asked for an explanation about something he had said in my back garden about Iram. He denied it and tried to cover it up. He lied to my face. His lies brought the truth about him to light, and my positive perceptions of him started fading. I began to see his reality clearly.

As I processed his behaviour over the two years of our friendship, he called me to say he was getting married in Pakistan and asked if he could borrow five grand from me because he needed money for the wedding. He only told me about his wedding because he wanted to ask for money. I couldn't believe what he was asking after all his lies and disloyalty. Now I realised why he had previously mentioned having a difficult time and implying I would help him. He was trying to manipulate me into believing I needed to give him money when he asked, so I would be unable to refuse. But I had taken control of my mind and refused to let others manipulate me. I gave him a clear "no" for the money.

He was rushing into marriage without even meeting the girl due to his fear of infatuation and getting bored. Instead of finding and healing the real reason for his behaviour, he decided to marry as quickly as possible before getting bored, not realising what he would do when he got bored after marriage.

Because he was a confused and complicated man, there were many reasons behind his actions, feelings, and thoughts. One reason for getting married was that he wanted the girl to rescue him, save him, take away his misery and financial struggles, and even take away his attachments to me. He did not realise that we attract romantic partners with the same vibration we have. A miserable and desperate person will attract another miserable and desperate person, and when two miserable people meet, their misery multiplies, just as when two joyful people meet, joyfulness multiplies. My friendship with him was dying, and I knew he would never listen to me, so I just told him, one last time, that I suggested he get married after healing himself.

I remembered asking him once if I could come to his house with the kids for the weekend, as he had never invited me to his new house, and he said no, making an excuse that his friend's wife was living there with her baby. He believed that loved ones leave eventually, so he did not want to put any effort into our friendship. He put very little effort into our friendship, believing I would leave him one day. His low self-esteem also prevented him from treating me well, as he felt intimidated by me.

It took me some time to gain clarity about his behaviour. When he noticed I was pulling away from him, he rang me. That day, he started talking with full energy and attention, like he used to in the beginning. But by then, it was too late. My energy was not the same, and I ended the call as I could not talk. He decided to talk with full energy and attention to regain my full attention because he was an avoidant co-dependent.

40

I was giving him the unconditional love, care, and respect he craved from a woman. He was not attached to me but to what he was getting from me. At the same time, he hated me because I was too strong, confident, and bold for him. My light reminded him of his darkness. My happiness reminded him of his misery. My sense of being enough reminded him of his feelings of inadequacy. His pain came from his low self-esteem and his own wounds and blocks, but his mind misinterpreted that pain and told him I was the reason for it. He wanted to unload his pain onto me.

He started getting jealous of me and tried to bring me down by making me feel bad. He attempted to make me feel bad since he came back into my life, but in very subtle ways. When he noticed he couldn't make me feel bad, he lied and used Iram's situation to make me feel jealous and lower my vibration.

He had no idea who I was. As Osho says, "Higher can understand lower, but lower cannot understand higher." If I feel jealous, I will sit with my jealousy and work on where it is coming from. I will find the root cause of my jealousy because jealousy is not about the other person. It comes from believing in your inner lack.

A true friend will never feel negative about their friend based on someone else's words. If he felt negative about me after listening to Iram, it means he doesn't truly know me. A friend who doesn't know me, lies to me, and tries to make me feel bad has no right to be my friend. I decided to end our friendship.

He called me again a few days later, and I told him everything I had come to understand about him. He didn't say anything for the first few minutes, then accused me of judging him. I told him I was speaking my truth and that I could forgive him but would never forget. I ended the call and blocked his number.

I didn't have any attachment or high expectations from him, so I wasn't hurt this time. However, something broke inside me, and that was my trust. My trust in him shattered. I told Rajni that I was so glad she was in my life and that if she weren't, my trust in humanity would be broken. Then I realised it was my blind trust that had been broken by Rohan, which needed to be broken for me to gain clarity.

I thought I was helping him, but I had no idea he came into my life to teach me very important life lessons, one of which was breaking my blind trust in people. I had a deep, unhealthy pattern of trusting people blindly without letting them earn my trust. I learned this blind trust to survive in my childhood when I couldn't trust my own mother. To avoid the pain of broken trust, I developed a pattern of blind trust.

In my personal growth journey, I had often heard and read that trust needs to be earned, but I could never break my pattern until now. Rohan was honest in financial matters, returning the money he borrowed even after I blocked him. I never had any money-related issues in our friendship.

I was expecting honesty, loyalty, and faithfulness, which he never had. He showed me red flags at the beginning of our friendship during Raham's illness, but I wasn't able to see them. He was wounded, not honest with himself, and his trust in humanity, especially in women, was broken. This is why he couldn't see my sincerity and loyalty and couldn't trust me.

He got confused by my unconditional love. He was under the illusion that, no matter what he did, I would love him. He didn't know that unconditional love in friendship and relationships must be earned. The price for unconditional love is honesty, loyalty, sincerity, truthfulness, being open and transparent, and an equal exchange of loving energy and respect. Without that foundation, unconditional love cannot survive.

He had no idea that if I can love someone unconditionally, I can also love them from a distance if they don't share my values. After blocking Rohan, I spent many months processing the reasons for his behaviour. I was curious to understand his complicated behaviour and the reasons behind his confusion, so I delved deep into his psyche. I started gaining insights into the reasons behind his behaviour and where his patterns were coming from.

I wanted to understand the reason for his resentment towards me and had the insight that he was still romantically fantasising about me. He went on holiday with us, hoping to get "something." When he didn't get what he was expecting, his resentment grew. But that was just his mind giving him an excuse for his resentment. The actual reason was buried deep in his subconscious.

When his dad left, his mum remarried, and his stepdad used to physically torture him. As a child, he expected his mum to protect him, which she couldn't do. He blamed all his pain on his mum for not protecting him and providing him with safety, so he started resenting and hating her for that.

The resentment and disgust he showed me were actually directed at his mum, which he was projecting onto me. He would project this pain onto every woman without realising it. Because his mum didn't save him, he had an intense desire for her to save him. He projected this desire onto other women, expecting them to rescue, provide for, love, and nurture him—needs that his mum didn't fulfil. These desires created unrealistic expectations of women, while at the same time, he resented them. He asked to borrow money not because he was greedy or wanted to exploit me financially, but because he had unrealistic expectations and a dependency on me.

I met his mum, and she had many qualities. However, because of his resentment, he couldn't see or appreciate those qualities and claimed she was a narcissist without truly understanding narcissism. Rohan's stepdad died when he was ten, and his mum raised her kids as a single working mother. She tried her best to provide a good life for them financially, sending them to good private schools and college in Pakistan. She even sent Rohan to the UK with her own money for his education.

I believe a child's safety should be a mother's priority, but I also understand how challenging and difficult it can be to be a single mother in Pakistan. Rohan's mum's mistakes can be forgiven. He can only give and receive love from women if he acknowledges and processes his pain, forgives his mum, and connects to his own source of love.

43

Lies, cheating, and disloyalty weren't deeply ingrained in his psyche. He learned those behaviours as coping mechanisms to survive in an emotionally abusive and toxic relationship for many years. Because leaving his toxic partner wasn't an option in his mind, he started seeking distractions through cheating and lying.

He compromised his integrity to save his toxic marriage. Although the marriage didn't last, his spirit was broken. He can reclaim his dignity, honesty, and spirit through healing.

I also learned that it's not just narcissistic people who hurt others; any wounded person can cause harm.

After gaining a deep understanding of his behaviour, I no longer felt the need to forgive him for what he did during our friendship. Instead, I felt compassion for him. I believe he is an amazing soul and, as an empath, he has many gifts and talents he could share with the world if he heals himself.

My last words to him were, "I will forgive you, but I will never forget what you did to me." Though I said this unconsciously, I was right. I have forgiven him, but I will never forget his lies, manipulations, and attempts to bring me down despite my consistent love, care, respect, and nurturing energy.

I learned another lesson from him: to forgive but not to forget the wrongs done to me. I was not just an over-giver; I was an over-forgiver as well. I had a pattern of forgetting the wrong behaviour, even abuse, and treating my abuser with the same niceness and trust, despite the emotional and psychological damage they had caused me in the past. By doing so, I was giving many chances to my abuser to hurt me again.

I learned that we should forgive, as grudges, anger, and hatred poison our own being and lower our vibrations. But we should never forget the abuse, manipulations, lies, and gaslighting of our abuser so that we do not allow them or others to repeat that cycle again.

One reason I became friends with my youngest son's dad, Haris, was forgetting the pain and emotional abuse. While writing this book, I remembered everything he did because I had forgiven him and held no grudges. Now, I recall everything without any pain or anger. My friendship with Haris was already fading due to my personal growth and vibrational mismatch with him. After remembering his abuse, my friendship with him nearly ended. I still respect him, and I need to talk to him to a certain extent because of our son.

I have reached a point where I have zero tolerance for any kind of abuse, lies, manipulation, or gaslighting in my life. I am okay with letting anyone go from my life who does not share my values, and I believe the universe will send me new people who align more closely with my values if I need them.

While I was learning the lessons from Rohan's behavior, my mind was becoming cynical and about to get believe that there are no good men in this world. My consciousness had dialogue with my mind. My mind said, there is no even one honest, loyal and trustworthy man you have ever came across so far, even as friend you fond disloyal man, so all men are untrust worthy. My consciousness said, there are good man out there. Honest loyal and trustworthy. You even know many men through books, social media and they are doing great work for humanity. My mind said, but they are only on screen, you have not met any honest man in real. My consciousness said, it does not matter if I only know them through screen, they exist on this earth right now. Then my mind went quiet and surrendered to my consciousness.

I know by heart that there are good men out there, who have dignity, integrity, loyalty, faithfulness and they know how to provide, protect, love, respect and treat women like a queen.

Raham's treatment finished in October, and he improved, but he was still not well enough to go to school or live a normal life. He never became violent with me again, but he still gets agitated, angry, and sometimes violent with his brothers. Handling him and being patient with him is not a problem for me.

Discontentment and Forgiveness Towards My Mum

After resolving my issues with Rohan, I asked my guides again to show me my blind spot. In the next few days, I started feeling a sense of discontentment. Initially, it was a subtle feeling, and my mind began to misinterpret it, suggesting that I would feel content when I found my "Mr Right." For a few days, I was confused, and my mind kept telling me to find romantic love to achieve contentment. However, I did not listen to my mind because I knew that I had done all the work regarding romantic love and that this feeling of something missing was not due to the absence of a romantic partner in my life.

I started meditating on it. Some feelings were buried so deep within me that I struggled for a few days to access them. One day, while sitting on my sofa waiting for a client, I felt the urge to meditate. As I sat in meditation, I saw my raw self again, and this time, more deeply. I accessed a deep sense of disconnection and frustration. This discontentment was not from my recent life; it had been buried within me for many years and many lifetimes.

As I accessed, felt, and acknowledged those feelings, the discontentment and frustration within me vanished in a few minutes. When I came out of meditation, that discontentment had turned into deep contentment, and the frustration into peace.

I was surprised to realise how disconnected and dissociated we can be from ourselves, not knowing what unprocessed feelings and blocks we carry within us. My mind had been telling me to find romantic love, thinking that a relationship would give me contentment, which was false and delusional. I came to the realisation that no one can take away the feeling of discontentment within me. In fact, if I enter a relationship carrying deep discontentment, not even the healthiest person on the planet can fill that gap within me, and that relationship will trigger my discontentment because relationships are mirrors.

After finding contentment and deep peace within myself, I realised I had forgiven my mum. Next day when I finely fond peace within, my niece, Aqsa, told me she visited my mum because my mum wanted to see her. Aqsa said my mum had a stroke and asked for forgiveness. She said she forgave my mum and sent me a short video my mum made for me.

When I saw my mum after many years, she looked so old, frail, and sick. She had no teeth and was almost bedridden because of the stroke. In the video, she was asking how I was and how my kids were while struggling to talk.

Aqsa told me my mum is struggling financially as my brothers are not doing well and cannot provide her with proper medical treatment or good food. For the first time, I felt compassion for my mum and forgave her for everything. I told Aqsa I would send money for my mum every month until she is no longer with us, which Aqsa can give to her. However, I still don't feel like talking to my mum, and I validate my feelings by not speaking to her, but I am sending her money regularly.

As a mother, I know how hard it is to carry a child for nine months, give birth, and take care of an infant. By just being a mum, she deserves something from me. Whatever she did was an unconscious act. She was wounded and in pain, projecting what she had inside her.

The Broken Faith

I had been suffering from hay fever for a few years. One day, I woke up with very bad hay fever, sneezing continuously. I sat in a meditation position, trying to meditate, but I couldn't focus due to my runny nose and sneezing. I got fed up with my hay fever and started begging God to fix it. This time, I wasn't praying—I was begging, like a professional beggar, and I was mourning.

Then I heard a voiceless voice in my head, like a clear thought: "Okay, but you do not need to beg and cry." Those words were comforting and humorous. I paused for a moment and smiled, realising I was praying in my old religious way, where we were taught to beg and ask for mercy from God.

I came to the realisation of my old prayer templates. Then I had a little dialogue, like talking to a best friend. I said with a smile on my face, "Oh yes, I don't have to beg, but please can you heal my hay fever?" Then I heard, "Healing can happen, prayers can be answered, but do you have faith?"

I replied, "I don't know, but I know you can heal me." The response was: "I made you with my own reflection, and you can heal and manifest anything with your own healing powers and faith. Do you have that unwavering faith where not even a single doubt arises in your mind?"

After hearing this, I sat in meditation with the intention of examining my faith. What I saw with my inner eyes and conscious awareness was broken faith: my broken faith in myself, in God, and in the universe (the law of the universe), and many doubts.

I was surprised to realise that despite my broken faith, I had taken many leaps of faith, and the universe had never disappointed me. I wondered what I could achieve and manifest if I had unwavering faith—the possibilities seemed endless.

I started working on strengthening my faith and discovered that faith is like a muscle: with continuous work and effort, you can make it strong. Faith also needs training—knowing how, when, and where to have unwavering faith. My faith is stronger than before, and I am working towards achieving unwavering faith.

Since I was able to observe my own faith, I can see the faith of others and have found that the majority of people are walking on this earth with broken faith. The level of broken faith varies: some people have more broken faith than others, and some have extremely broken faith in themselves, humanity, and the universe.

Scarcity Mindset

On 1st January 2024, when I saw this date on the calendar, I had an intuition that this year would be my year of manifestations. I also had an insight that I had a scarcity mindset and needed to work on making it an abundant mindset to manifest abundance in my life.

This made me realise I didn't truly know myself. I thought that because I had no attachments to money, it was enough to attract abundance in my life. But I needed to think and believe in abundance to attract it.

My mother had a deep attachment to money, and I could sense it if anyone had attachments to money. My whole family suffered because of my mum's attachment to money. I realised at a young age that attachments to money were not good. However, I did have a few blocks regarding money, and I had been working on them since my awakening. But the awareness of a scarcity mindset was clear and loud.

Working on my blocks without conscious awareness never proved effective. Until my awareness shone a light on my block, and I became fully aware of it, as one rule of healing is: if you cannot see it, you cannot heal it.

I started working on rewiring my neural network to cultivate an abundant mindset by saying daily affirmations about abundance, money, and success, and by thinking and believing that we live in an abundant world where there is always enough for everyone.

The Chaser in Me

I realised, without asking, that my body and mind were set in chase mode, and I needed to let go of that chaser in me to manifest my dreams. I observed the chasing energy within me. Chasing energy implies lack—it means I am lacking something, which is why I am chasing it. This very chasing mindset and energy push our goals away.

It did not take many days for me to let go of the chasing energy. After releasing the chaser within me, I felt at ease, realising I don't have to run to manifest my goals.

I read in the book "The Seven Spiritual Laws of Success" by Deepak Chopra that one law of the universe is the law of least effort. He wrote, "This law is based on the fact that nature's intelligence functions with effortless ease and abandoned carefreeness. This is the principle of least action, of no resistance."

After letting go of the chaser within me, I deleted the dating app and stopped chasing romantic love. There is nothing wrong with finding love, but I was not just looking for love—I was chasing it for many years, and it was time to let go. I believe that what is meant for me will come to me in its divine time.

The Book

After Rajni's vision about my book in 2022, I never thought about it again until January 2024 arrived, and I had no idea where to start. I was in limbo when I saw an advert on social media about books selling on Amazon. I signed up for a master class, and while I was watching the hour-long session, my mind kept telling me I was wasting my time. I wondered why a hairdresser like me would try to sell books on Amazon. Yet, something compelled me to sit and watch that master class. Soon after, ads about books, sales, publishing, and marketing started appearing on my phone.

I told Rajni that I felt like the universe was giving me a signal to write a book, but my mind kept saying it wasn't the right time. Rajni encouraged me, saying it was indeed the time to start writing. A few days later, she told me she had seen a vision of my two books and explained that I would write a second part of my autobiography. One thing led to another, and I began writing my book.

Giving Up the Mind

While writing, I asked my guides to show me my blind spots again. In the next few days, I had the feeling of being stuck. This feeling had been with me for many years, but I was not fully aware of it. I used to feel that my life was not moving as it should. The more I meditated on it, the clearer it became that it was my mind that felt stuck. Since my awakening, my life was led by my soul, not my mind. My mind felt stuck because my life was not unfolding according to its plans. Despite seven years of awakening and healing by 2024, my mind kept telling me I was doing well yet had not manifested any goals or dreams, while others seemed successful after only four or five years of their healing and awakening.

One day, while writing a chapter of my book, I felt an intense urge to give up. After fully experiencing this feeling, I realised it was not me but my mind telling me to give up. I told my mind, "You give up; I will never give up." That day, my mind relinquished control of my life, and the feeling of being stuck vanished.

My mind had been creating a block for my manifestations by feeling stuck. The very feeling of being stuck is a block, as our minds do not realise that merely wishing, imagining, and getting attached cannot attract what we need. Wishing and getting attached, followed by feeling stuck, create blocks to our manifestations.

My body and soul had been aligning over the past few months, but my mind was taking its time. By relinquishing control, I felt ease and openness, and my mind began to align with my soul and body.

Courage, Comfort, and Drive

Rajni told me she had been informed in her meditation that her soul's name is Comfort and mine is Courage, indicating that her main soul gift and essence is comfort, while mine is courage. This resonates with us. Rajni's true vibration is comfort. She is my biggest support and source of comfort in my life. Simply sitting with her brings me comfort. Her other spiritual gifts, such as receiving messages from other realms and her healing energy, also provide comfort to humanity.

I have always had courage within me, and this courage, stemming from my soul, has helped me overcome life's hardships, even when I lacked faith. I am a source of courage in Rajni's life. If her courage does not come from within, I am here to provide it. Because she fully trusts me, she draws courage from me whenever she needs it.

We are meant to share our soul's gifts with the world, but during our spiritual awakening, we truly needed each other, as awakening and coming into our power is not an easy journey. Rajni and I faced much opposition during our awakening and still do. We are focused on our healing journey, and many people dislike us without knowing the real reason—they dislike us because our light reminds them of their darkness. Instead of going within and finding their own light, they project their pain onto us.

Coming from a South Asian background, men believe they are superior to women and that women should serve them. As Rajni and I come into our personal power and become strong women, the men around us feel threatened and intimidated, their egos hurt because we can no longer be controlled or manipulated. We do not nag, complain, or seek men's attention, nor do we believe we are lesser than men.

We also face opposition from women who think their way of living is the only right way. As Rajni and I break free from traditional programming, they feel insecure and threatened. In reality, everyone wants to live in freedom—freedom from old programming, traumas, wounds, and limitations. When we cannot claim our freedom, we envy others who have. Rajni and I not only faced our own demons but also others' demons, which helped us become stronger.

Our circle has become smaller, as healing is a lonely journey. We are fortunate to have each other on the same path, to understand, comfort, and encourage one another. My courage is not just for Rajni and me; one of my soul purposes is to give courage to humanity for their healing and evolution.

I have discovered not only my shadows but also my soul's gifts and essence. I am driven to serve humanity. As a lightworker, I feel compelled to help humanity through healing.

Chapter 9 – Lessons Learned

I am Enough So Are You

One of the biggest lies a human can buy into is, "I am not enough." Unfortunately, most of the of people live under the illusion that they are not enough, without even realising it.

I am lucky that I did not have this belief very deeply, although I still experienced a lack of self-worth and self-love. When my first husband tried to make me believe that I was not enough, I realised the pain of that feeling. That is why I can understand the pain of others who have a very deep belief that they are not enough. I can see, feel, and sense how "I am not enough-ness" reflects in their feelings, thoughts, and actions.

We adopt this belief in our childhood, often growing up in abusive environments where our emotional needs are not met. We can even take on this belief when we are adults, from people who believe they are not good enough and project their belief onto others. Believing that "I am not enough" ruins our self-esteem, lowers our vibrations, makes us feel discontent, and disconnects us from our true selves.

I have closely witnessed people with the "I am not enough" belief and how it affects their relationships, friendships, and even professional lives. I realised this when I was treating certain people in my life with special care, love, and respect, but because they did not feel enough within themselves, nothing was enough for them. The feeling of "I am not enough" not only becomes a barrier to seeing our own self-worth and blessings, but it also prevents us from seeing and appreciating the love and effort of others towards us.

People who do not feel enough within themselves, when they have a close relationship with someone who feels confident and enough within themselves, try to make them feel not enough. They attempt to ruin the self-esteem of that person, and if they fail, they feel frustrated and defeated.

"I am not enough" not only makes us feel less and small, but it also complicates our lives. With low self-esteem and feelings of inadequacy, we do not even want to accept that we have self-esteem issues. Accepting this means feeling the pain of "I am not enough," and we do not want to feel pain. We want to run from pain.

Believing that "I am not enough," people openly or secretly compare themselves with others in their minds and feel small in front of people who are more confident and doing well in their lives. To avoid their pain, their minds project that pain onto others, which is how they sabotage their relationships and friendships. Narcissistic people adopt a persona to protect themselves from the pain of low self-esteem, while codependent people adopt different personas to avoid their pain.

Codependent people have a need to be needed, which stems from low self-esteem. They feel competent when they feel needed and like to surround themselves with people who take advantage of others. Then, they feel used, abused, and manipulated.

I realised how wounds make us selfish. The more wounded you are, the more selfish you become, whether you are codependent or narcissistic. Most of our actions that come from old wounds, traumas, and low self-esteem are based on selfishness. We do favours and over-give to make ourselves feel superior to others.

Ironically, even educated people do not know about self-esteem issues and how they can affect their lives, as our traditional education system does not teach important personal growth life skills. I teach my kids important life skills and constantly remind them, "You are smart enough, intelligent enough, good enough in your own unique way. If you exist in this vast existence, it means you matter, as creation does not make mistakes."

Human beings have the potential to make themselves as small as they want or to grow to the highest potential a human can evolve, reaching enlightenment. Believing that "I am not enough" will always make you feel small and inadequate, whether you have good friends, relationships, money, or success. In fact, achieving money, success, and relationships without feeling enough and content within yourself leads to more emptiness and hopelessness. The mind tells us that we will feel enough when we find a relationship or when we attract money and success. But when we achieve these, our mind tells us to chase something else or that there is no hope. The truth is, there is always hope, but our physical mind cannot comprehend it.

Reality is that we are enough, we are always enough, and we are so enough that we can make ourselves believe that we are not enough. "I am not enough" is just a belief, an energetic download in our system that dims our light, and we can claim our enoughness back at any time by knowing, accepting, and acknowledging that belief, processing the pain of not feeling enough, and then letting it go.

It is not that we must believe that we are enough; when we let go of the belief and delete the energetic download of "I am not enough" in our system, we will find that we are enough. "I am enough" is not a belief; it is knowing and realisation. A person who truly knows they are enough not only knows this about themselves but also recognises that everyone else is enough. Such a person will never make another person feel small or low.

The moment I realised I am enough, I understood that everyone is enough and that everyone has unique gifts and talents given by existence, which we can share with the world. I read in "Conversations with God," "life is not about you; your life is about everyone else's life you touch."

I Am Not My Ego

Growing up in Pakistan, I heard about ego maybe a few times in my entire life, as there is little discussion or understanding about ego. What I knew about ego was that people who are arrogant have ego. I never heard that there are many faces of ego and had no idea I was full of ego until my ego surrendered a little bit one day after coming through the dark night of the soul following my awakening. I witnessed my ego for the first time in 2019 and realised for the first time that I have an ego, but I am not my ego. For the first time, I witnessed the distance between my ego and my true self. Before that, I was living my life in survival mode, led by my ego.

I also realised my ego is not my enemy; it was trying to protect me from pain. I did not try to fight with my ego. Instead, I became loose and easy with life, and when I became loose and easy, I experienced the death of ego. We are all different, and everyone can deal with their ego in their own way. Understanding ego is very important to come out of the ego trap.

Ego comes online in our childhood to protect us from abusive environments, pain, and traumas. Even if there is no obvious abuse, ego still develops to give a sense of self. Ego gives us a mental construct and a false identity of who we think we are. When we are given traumas and wrong beliefs that we are not good enough, we feel shame, guilt, and fear because of the treatment we received as children. Then ego comes and gives us an illusionary sense of self and tells us that everything is okay and that if we do this and that, we will be good enough.

For a child, it is not possible to regulate the dense emotions caused by traumas, and it can be fatal for the child. Ego comes in childhood to save us. It is given by existence and serves us as children, but if we do not understand ego and let go of its control through understanding, it can become a big problem in our adulthood.

As I mentioned earlier, there are many faces of ego. Understanding which type of ego you have is key for personal growth. Narcissistic people have an ego that tells them they are better than others. They believe they should be treated specially. They compare themselves with others, criticise themselves, and their overactive mind keeps telling them, "You are stupid, you are ugly, you are lesser than others." Then their ego comes to tell them to prove to the world that they are smarter than anyone, more intelligent than anyone, and so on.

A healthy attitude is knowing that you are good enough in your own unique way, but thinking that you are better than others comes from ego. Ego reminds you of this because behind this ego, you are in pain from past wounds, emotionally broken, and unable to regulate your emotions. When you cannot regulate your emotions, you are emotionally immature and do not know how to protect yourself, so you need your ego to protect you. That is why they say, "narcissists are two-year-old children in adult bodies," and that is true. For them, the world is a scary place, and people are untrustworthy, so they carry a mask of ego to hide their brokenness, appearing strong, confident, and even charming.

I had what I call "the good girl" ego, which is harder to detect, and there are not many discussions about that ego. When I first became aware of my ego, it was a turning point in my life. There are men who have "the good boy" ego too. The good girl and good boy ego are more damaging to themselves than to others. That ego tells us to sacrifice, ignore our own needs and desires, and please others to get validation that we are good. It tells us not to speak up for ourselves; otherwise, people will think we are bad. It tells us to treat ourselves as doormats, to have no boundaries, no sense of self, so people think we are humble. Behind this humbleness, there is ego working in a sneaky way, hard to detect for the average person. Unless you are awakened and know your own ego, it is not easy to detect the good girl or good boy ego.

I remember one of my clients, who was also having her spiritual awakening, told me that her in-laws' family were talking badly about her, and all her life she was listening to this silently. Then one day, she got angry and had the courage to speak up for herself. Then she told me that she caught her ego and went quiet. I told her she did the right thing to get angry at the wrong treatment and speak up for herself, and that was not her ego. Her ego was what told her not to speak up for herself and to be nice so people would not turn against her.

I told her there are many types of ego, and she has the good girl ego. She was surprised to learn that, and it was her "awe" moment. Knowing her ego was a turning point in her personal growth.

To check the "good one" ego, we can review our lives honestly and assess if we are "nice" to everyone, including those who are weaker and in lower positions than us. By honestly reviewing, we can easily identify differences in our behaviour with various people. I have observed that as I became a healthier and stronger version of myself, some people around me assumed I did not need any help or favour because I do not expect, manipulate, or play the victim to get help. At the same time, those people pleasers are over-giving to those around them who manipulate and have huge expectations from them.

We might be pleasing narcissistic people or those who may appear stronger and manipulative, while at the same time, we seem frustrated and irritable with our kids and with people who do not demand anything from us. Ego wears different masks in front of different people. With some, it feels threatened, even without an actual threat, and it tries to protect us, while with others, it tells us to take out our frustration on them.

First, we are traumatised, hypnotised, and stripped of our authentic selves. Then our ego comes online to protect us, and subsequently, manipulative authoritative people use that very ego to manipulate us. It is the ego and mind that can be manipulated; the true self can never be manipulated.

Manipulative authoritative people have created numerous false beliefs, ideas, and judgements about human niceness and badness in society, which have been passed on to new generations for thousands of years, with new additions as well. They say, if you wear certain clothes, you are nice. If you sacrifice yourself for others, you are nice. If you live your life for others, you are nice. If you do not have any sense of self, you are nice and humble. If you perform certain religious practices, you are nice.

If you express your anger, you are bad. If women wear certain clothes, they are bad. If we speak up about our abusive parents, we are bad. If we live our lives according to our own terms and conditions, we are bad, and the list goes on.

The good girl or good boy ego does not want to hear that we are not nice because of their fear of judgement. We always try to fit into a false image of ourselves, which is given by someone else. This forces us to do things that make us nice to others, and we live in the delusion that one day people will acknowledge how nice we are. I was in that delusion, and when I started seeing reality clearly, I found out that people rarely say you are nice. Manipulative people think we are stupid, and people who cannot see themselves are unable to see others' efforts and sacrifices.

This ego trap is all about us. When we do certain things, our ego gets satisfaction, and the people who manipulate us to do these things also get ego satisfaction. This ego satisfaction mimics temporary happiness, and we think we are happy by doing things for others or by manipulating others. But that is not happiness at all. Ego satisfaction is momentary happiness. The ego is very fragile and can be hurt by small things. If someone praises you and your ego gets happy, the next moment, they criticise you, and your ego gets hurt, leaving you in pain.

Living your life with ego is living at the mercy of others. Hence, people are frustrated, unhappy, and struggle in relationships. Without healing and certain awareness, we cannot connect and have relationships with other human beings. It would be a relationship between two egos.

Ego is a barrier between us and our authentic selves, between us and our relationships, and between us and God. But the question is, how can we come out of our ego? We can come out of our ego by becoming aware of which type of ego we have. By observing our thoughts, feelings, and actions, and asking ourselves where they are coming from—are they coming from my ego?

Osho says, "Ego is an illusion, and ego is there because you are not there." By "you are not there," he means your consciousness is not present, your higher self is not there, so your lower self—your ego—is leading your life.

Ego is a mask that hides our wounded, broken self. Do not be afraid to face the broken parts of you, no matter how painful they can be. Because if we cannot see it, we cannot heal it through loving and soothing affirmations and by reminding ourselves we do not need the ego to protect us.

Ego does not die in one episode. The more we heal ourselves and become aware of our ego and its tactics, the smaller it will get. Ego gives the identity of "I am." Osho says, "The ego intrinsically dies on the fifth plane; 'I' dies but 'am-ness' still persists." Ego dies completely at the highest ladder of evolution a soul can reach, and only spiritual masters on this planet have reached that ladder. So, we do not need to expect our ego to die completely. I still have ego, although it is subtle now. I see my own ego occasionally.

My saviour complex and deep desires to save others were also coming from my ego. My ego wanted to give others the impression of "the great me." After letting go of those ego desires to save others, I found a healthy drive to help humanity, which comes from unconditional love and the understanding that we are all connected.

Less ego means more connection with our authentic self. The more connection we have with our authentic self, the more peace and contentment we find within. With that peace, we do not feel the need for external happiness. As mature adults, we do not need our ego to protect us, and we do not need to prove to anyone how good we are. It is about being authentic and honest with yourself and others.

Our true authentic self can never harm anyone. It is our wounds, unprocessed emotional pain, and ego that can cause harm to another human. Because our true nature is love, by connecting to our true selves, healing, and coming out of the ego trap, we do not need to protect ourselves by wearing the mask of the good girl or good boy or by behaving in a narcissistic way.

Gaining the ability to see my own ego and the ego of others, and knowing that I have an ego but am not my ego, was one of the most important life lessons I learned after my spiritual awakening.

I Am Not My Mind

The first time I glimpsed the awareness that I am not my mind was when I realised the manipulations of my second husband and how my mind had been controlled by his mind. It was a turning point in my life when I decided to take control of my mind.

What I have learned over many years of my spiritual awakening and observing my mind and the minds of people around me is that our mind is not designed to do the work we are taking from it. Our mind should not be the boss of our life; our mind should be the guard, and our consciousness or soul should be the boss of our life. But when our consciousness is asleep, our mind takes charge of our life.

The mind can be corrupted with false beliefs and ideas from society, parents, and people around us, which go deep into our subconscious mind. The mind starts projecting those beliefs and ideas into our current reality. It sees reality through the lenses of the past. Unless we clean our mind of all the junk that has been installed in it, we will not be able to see reality as it is.

If someone's trust is broken in humanity, the mind takes the belief that no one is trustworthy, and it will never trust anyone even if they meet many trustworthy people in their life. The mind filters reality according to our past wounds, traumas, and experiences, misjudges situations, people, and feelings, and with that misjudgement, it sabotages relationships and friendships.

For example, people with deep unprocessed pain, when their pain is triggered by certain people, the mind misinterprets that trigger and tells us that they are the reason for our pain. To protect us from pain, the mind starts telling us ways to unload our pain on others.

Our consciousness is the source of intelligence, not the mind, especially when it is corrupted. Our mind is not able to tell us that we have no self-love and sense of self-worth, or that we have old wounds and pains that need healing. Our higher self gives us insights about our blind spots and wounds if we sit, relax, and allow ourselves to listen to it.

Many people make the mistake every day of unloading their pain on others because their mind tells them it is others who are causing them pain by triggering them. Triggers are good and are signs that there is something we need to heal. Instead of projecting our pain on others, we need to go within and heal the very wound and pain that is being triggered by someone.

It is the mind's job to protect us from pain and bring our focus to pleasure. This is its survival mechanism; it helps us survive in a chaotic environment. However, when we are adults and still live in survival mode, it becomes a problem. When something triggers us, we feel pain, and the mind will tell us to unload our pain on others, seek distractions, or engage in unhealthy activities to gain pleasure.

Unloading pain on others and seeking distractions might temporarily divert us from pain, but it can sabotage our relationships, and the mind cannot comprehend the consequences.

The mind also likes to hold onto something to feel in control of life. It can even hold onto suffering. I do not just love reading myself; I love reading other people, and I know a few people in my life who are addicted to their suffering and even enjoy it. Although we all want a happy life consciously, they suffer because of their subconscious mind. The strange thing is that these people may not have any significant suffering or struggle in their current life; they are suffering because of their past and their mind.

One part of them is fed up with suffering, while their mind is enjoying it. They will not find a way out until they go within, take charge of their life from the mind, and live with conscious awareness.

The mind is a powerful tool given by existence, and if used consciously, we can manifest happiness and bliss. If it can manifest suffering, why not manifest abundance and peace? To manifest abundance, happiness, and peace, we need to declutter our mind and expand our consciousness so we can see reality without any filters.

I learnt that I cannot fight against my mind; instead, I need to understand it. I remember at the beginning of my awakening, whenever I noticed my mind freaking out or telling me to distract myself from pain, I used to say, "Dear mind, it is okay; I can face the pain now. Dear mind, it is okay; you do not need to protect me." It worked, and after saying these affirmations a few times, it would stop giving me those wrong suggestions.

I started by taking baby steps to take control of my life from my mind. Through meditation, healing, and understanding how the universe and my mind work, after seven years, my mind gave up. It relinquished some of its control, and I found an ease in life that I had never felt before.

The mind loves to make things complicated so it feels competent by trying to solve many things at once, which should not be problems in the first place. Our mind uses our vital energy by creating problems, then trying to solve them, by planning the future, thinking about the past, and unnecessarily cluttering our thoughts, leaving little energy for the rest of our body to function. That is why people seem unnecessarily tired.

Gaining the ability to watch, observe, and understand my mind gave me the realisation that I have a mind, but I am not my mind. I can use my mind according to my own will, and I can even create new neurological pathways and activate dormant parts to make my brain work more efficiently.

I Am Responsible

When I separated from my first husband, my mind told me that if I married again and found a good man, my life would be perfect. So, I was giving all my responsibilities to my second husband to make me happy. When this did not work, I learned my lesson and understood that my happiness is my responsibility. I am responsible for my happiness and even my misery. Transformation started happening within me by taking responsibility for my life.

It is easy to blame others for our misery and make others responsible for our happiness, but life becomes difficult with that approach. The truth is no one is responsible for our happiness and misery. We are responsible for everything in our life. We manifest people, situations, and circumstances according to our wounds, traumas, vibration levels, mindset, heart set, and soul set.

I learnt that I need to take responsibility for my mind and be aware of what other people are trying to make me think and believe by putting their thoughts into my mind to make me act and behave in certain ways according to their own agendas. Some people will plant certain seeds of thought in our minds so we will act according to their expectations of us.

I went on a few dates with a man whom I found to be a narcissist after a few dates. On our last date, he said a few things to make me feel he was not sure about me, and then he said with full energy and acted happiness that he saw something in my eyes. He was so convincing that a few years ago, the naïve me would have believed it. But now, I was aware enough to see that he wanted me to believe that I loved him so I would act and behave as if I loved him, even if I did not. I also knew that love does not come from the mind; it comes from the heart, and if I love someone, I will know. I understood his manipulation and said no to him anyway. Since I took responsibility for my mind, I have become more aware of how people try to use our own minds for their benefit.

I have one client who has been married for 25 years and has been blaming her husband for her misery for the entire duration. She thinks that if her husband changes, her life will improve. I have reminded her repeatedly that it is not her husband who needs to change; she does. Only then will her life change. However, she is so stuck in her mind that she does not want to understand or take responsibility. She is comfortable in her discomfort and unconsciously knows that if she takes responsibility, she will have to face the discomfort.

There are millions of people on this planet who blame their partners, parents, kids, politicians, and the government for their happiness, suffering, misery, and financial struggles. Life will start to change for the better the day we take responsibility for our own lives.

Letting Go

One of the important lessons I learnt was to find your true self; you must be ready to let go of your old self, beliefs, ideas, and conditioning of the mind. We even need to let go of certain people or maybe most people in our lives, and that is scary for many. We do not just get attached to people, money, or material things; we also get attached to our identity, beliefs, and religious ideology.

Letting go of identity and beliefs borrowed from society can be scary. The mind wonders, "If I am not what I am, then who am I?" We do not want to jump into the unknown, and the mind keeps trying to hold on to a false identity.

I experienced the pain when my identity shattered in front of me. Then I realised why people do not awaken easily: finding your true self is not an easy journey and can be scary for many. Some people fight and even kill others for the sake of their identity and beliefs, not knowing that an identity needing protection through violence is false. Deep down, they have doubts and try to justify them, continually proving to others that they are right to suppress their doubts.

A person who knows their true self also knows the true selves of others and understands that we are all one and part of a divine plan, and there is nothing to fight about.

In the beginning, it can be scary, but if we manage to handle that feeling and take a leap of faith, even with our broken faith, the universe will always reward us.

We already have light within us; we already have our true selves and souls' gifts and essence. That true self and light get covered up with layers upon layers of beliefs, wounds, trauma, conditioning, and shadows.

Finding our true self and healing is about peeling away those layers. It has been referred to as peeling the layers of an onion because we are so attached to our old identity that sometimes it feels like ripping yourself apart, and it can be painful. Rajni and I have experienced this pain, but we have also experienced joy and true happiness after peeling each layer and letting go of an old self that never served us.

After letting go of all the unnecessary burdens I carried, I have found my individuality. Yes, there is more to know and more to let go of, and I am ready to let go of anything to find my light within me, even if it is painful and frightening.

God Is All That Is

"Whenever you are alone, remind yourself that God has sent everyone else away so that there is only you and him." - Rumi.

Growing up in an extremely chaotic and abusive environment, feeling lonely, unseen, and unheard, I always had a feeling that there was someone who listened to me, someone who cared about me. I always felt a subtle connection with God, even before my spiritual awakening, although I was given certain false beliefs about God.

After my spiritual awakening, the more I got to know myself, the more I connected with myself and God, discovering that God is not what I had been told.

A quote from Alan Watts states, "In order to come into full union with God, you must give up any conception of God whatsoever."

God is beyond the descriptions of words and the understanding of the mind. It is not about believing in God; it is about knowing God. We can feel God as divine source energy, and that divine source energy is all there is.

Osho says about God, "To me, God is existence, and existence is impersonal."

In my experience, we are all connected with God all the time. We are never separate from God. In "Conversations with God," writer Neale Donald Walsch asks, "To whom does God communicate? Are there special people? Are there special times?" The answer is, "All people are special, and all moments are golden."

Neale asks, "How do you communicate?" The answer is, "I communicate through feelings, thoughts, and words. Words are really the least effective communicator. They are most open to misinterpretation."

If ten years ago someone had told me that they could talk to God, I would have laughed because of my own blocks and programming. But now, I am not afraid to say that I can feel and connect to God. God communicates through feelings and thoughts most of the time. After meditating for many years, I have quieted my mind to a certain extent that I can differentiate whether thoughts come from my mind or from God, but only sometimes. God is always here and talks to us all the time, but my ability to talk to God is limited so far. For me, it is like playing hide and seek with God. Sometimes I can listen and feel God's messages, but sometimes I get stuck in my mind.

I have learned that life is meant to be lived and enjoyed, not taken too seriously. So, I am enjoying the process of playing hide and seek with God. We are not going anywhere. There is no race and no rush; that is the beauty, and life is a gift.

One afternoon, I had an intense urge to visit my next-door neighbour, who is also my friend. I went to her house and saw her very depressed and sad as she had just finished crying. I told her that I had a message for her and felt like saying, "God loves you unconditionally." She told me that the other day she was complaining to God and feeling that God did not care about her. She said my message gave her comfort and hope that she is not alone and that God loves her. She has never forgotten that. God can talk to us through other people.

My friend Rajni has her own soul's gift and way of communicating with God. Because she is good at meditation and can go deep into a thoughtless state, she communicates through her meditation. She has had a few dialogues with God, all about her healing, coming into her personal power, and learning to see others through God's eyes, which is with unconditional love and non-judgment.

Rajni and I are ordinary people, or if we are special, then everyone is special in God's eyes. Everyone can communicate with God if we can. Everyone can experience and feel God. To communicate with God, we must get rid of old programming and let go of the belief that God only talks to special people.

Finding the Balance

Before my awakening, I was at one extreme: an over-giver, over-forgiver, overly caretaker, overly polite and sweet, overly positive. I attracted people, especially romantic partners, who were at the other extreme.

At the beginning of my awakening, I became more positive, more giving, and more forgiving because I believed that spirituality was all about forgiving and sending blessings to others. Since I had no one physically in my life who was ahead in personal growth to learn from, I made many mistakes even after my awakening and learnt from them.

There is a misconception about spirituality and spiritual people: they should not get angry, complain, struggle, be strict, or be wealthy.

There are different levels of soul evolution and spirituality, and the highest level of spirituality and soul evolution is what I call the Buddha level. We cannot reach the Buddha level by bypassing all levels, emotions, and feelings.

I have a client; she and her husband are experiencing a spiritual awakening. They were at the initial stage of awakening when she told me a story about a person who betrayed her and caused her financial loss. My client was sad, upset, and angry about her financial loss and betrayal. When she was telling me the story, I could feel her sadness, and to me, she had the right to be sad, angry, and feel betrayed. She needed time to process her emotions.

She told me that her husband advised her to understand that the woman who betrayed her came from an abusive family and to send her peace and blessings.

I told my client that what her husband was saying was bypassing her feelings and emotions. You cannot reach the higher ladder of spirituality by bypassing your feelings and emotions. She then asked me the most important question: how to find the balance?

I told her she needed to acknowledge and allow herself to feel and process her emotions and pain. Her question stuck in my mind: how to find balance?

I know many people who have been told to be good girls or good boys rather than authentic. Under the burden of parents' and society's expectations, we have forgotten who we are. We have forgotten how to find balance.

I wish someone had told me what type of ego and personality traits I had, which extreme I was at, so I could choose the correct path that leads to balance for me. There is no one path for everyone; there can be different paths for different individuals.

I was already an over-giver, and I read in Deepak Chopra's book "The Seven Spiritual Laws of Success." One law was the "Law of Giving." This book is one of my favourites and helped me so much in my personal growth, but when I read the law of giving, I did not fully understand it. I started saying the affirmation daily, "Today I will give something to everyone." I started giving more and had no idea where that giving was coming from. It was coming from my ego and lack of self-worth.

It took me many years to understand that first I needed to understand my ego, fill my own cup, and then serve humanity out of unconditional love, without expecting anything in return, not even praise or validation.

To find the balance for a good girl or good boy, we need to stop over-giving to gain validation. The good girl/good boy ego is hard to detect. Go within and keep your ego in check. We should not confuse ego satisfaction from giving with true happiness and joy from giving, which can only be felt when you feel whole and complete within yourself.

To find balance for a good girl or good boy, validate, own, and regulate your emotions and feelings. We should not force ourselves to forgive when we are not ready; instead, focus on healing. Learn to stand up for ourselves, speak up when necessary, block toxic people, move away from negativity without feeling guilty, and not sacrifice for anyone. Make ourselves a priority and do not be afraid to hear when people call us selfish. Connect to our inner peace, joy, and happiness. When our cup is overflowing, give without any expectation while being careful about who we surround ourselves with.

To find balance for negative and narcissistic people, they need to train their minds to find positivity in life and in others. There has been too much negativity and darkness on this planet, but the truth is, there are always honest, loyal people you can find. The universe will send you these honest and loyal people at some point in your life, but if we see reality through the filter of our mind, we cannot see positivity. You can train your mind to see reality as it is.

Narcissistic people have a block against giving. If they give, their giving comes from the ego mind to keep the other person on the hook. Watch and understand your ego, and start giving, even if it is small, without any expectation.

Watch your judgmental mind, and train your mind to be non-judgmental. Narcissism is a coping mechanism. When you go within and heal yourself, you will find your true self, which is nothing but love, peace, and abundance.

For me, balance is not being too positive or too negative. It is being authentic, honest, and true to ourselves in each given moment. It is not bypassing your emotions and not wearing any masks.

We Are Our Own Healer

One of the most important lessons I learnt from healing myself is that we are our own healer and our own guru. We can heal our traumas, blocks, and unhealthy behaviour in the comfort of our own homes.

We are living in the best time on Earth, and the planet is going through a major evolutionary process. Earth's vibration has been at a 3D level for thousands of years, which is a lower consciousness. The Earth's vibrations started changing in 2012, with new light codes arriving on Earth and shifting the vibration from 3D to 5D, which is a higher consciousness.

In 2023, I saw with my own eyes the difference in Earth's energy. I was lying down on the grass in my back garden and began to see Earth's energy, which was different from the energy I saw in 2020. The new energy was more condensed and vibrating at a higher speed.

This new Earth energy is also helping us to raise our vibrations and expand our consciousness. New light codes are helping us by bringing our shadows to the surface so we can see and heal them. This is why it is the best time to incarnate on Mother Earth, as the Earth is supporting us in healing and raising our consciousness.

If we resist working on ourselves and remain attached to our old programming, living on this Earth will become increasingly difficult for those people, due to the energetic difference between Mother Earth and people with 3D consciousness.

Another reason we are living in the best time on Earth is the advancement in technology and the exchange of information. We are so connected through technology that information can reach us within seconds from any part of the world.

How we use technology and what kind of information we consume depends on us. We can use technology for our highest good. We should be mindful of whom we follow, as there is so much content out there. There are amazing spiritual teachers, life coaches, and healers who are putting incredible work online from which we can learn and grow.

Rajni and I are healing ourselves in the comfort of our own home while living normal and busy lives. We read books that help us grow and expand our consciousness. We watch videos and follow spiritual teachers who assist us in our healing and growth.

Even if we learn from different people and seek guidance from life coaches, we must face our demons and heal ourselves. There is nobody who can rescue us; we need to rescue ourselves.

Meditation played a big part in our healing, ascension, and witnessing our own blind spots. Without meditation, Rajni and I would not be where we are today.

Just a few years ago, there was a concept that meditation was for monks or that you needed to leave regular life and go into isolation to meditate. What I learnt from my experience is that meditation is for everyone, especially in today's busy life when our minds cannot rest and keep running unnecessarily.

If I tell hundreds of people to meditate, only a few will do it, and I used to wonder why. Meditation is just sitting with yourself for a few minutes a day. Then I realised that people are afraid to go within; they are afraid to face their demons and repressed emotions, wounds, and traumas. The ego and mind also resist meditation, as it is the death of the ego and mind. The ego knows that when you start meditating, it will lose control of your life, so it will make a thousand and one excuses to stop you from meditating.

People with a hustling lifestyle and stressed minds will also struggle to meditate because their minds will tell them that sitting and doing nothing is wasting time. But I would say that sitting in meditation is the best use of time and the best gift you can give to yourself.

We all need meditation. It calms our minds, eliminates stress and depression, raises our vibration, heals us, and helps us escape the ego trap and mind control.

When we are disconnected from ourselves, we cannot connect with others, even with our children and with God. Meditation helps us to connect to ourselves, and the more connected we are with ourselves, the more connected we will be with others. We all want to be seen, heard, and understood, but the irony is that we are not seen, heard, and understood by ourselves. Until we see, hear, and understand ourselves, nothing will be enough from the outer world.

Meditation is the best way for healing and to find our true selves. Even if our minds and egos resist, if we keep meditating, one day they will surrender.

We humans are so powerful, strong, and supernatural. We have been conditioned to think small, act small, and be small. If we let that supernatural part of us, which is our healer too, take charge, we can heal anything and forgive anything.

Let the healer within you do its magic and become your own healer. If I can heal myself, you can do it too.

We Are All Guided

Growing up in the big, overpopulated city of Lahore as the unplanned seventh child out of nine, I believed that God sent souls to Earth randomly. I had no idea how the universe worked, and what I had been told through certain beliefs did not satisfy me. Deep down, I had my doubts and always had a curiosity to know more. Something within me was not comfortable with the borrowed beliefs I had been given, so I kept searching. After some misinformation and choosing the wrong paths, I eventually found the right track and information that resonated with me. Through my heart, intuition, and direct downloads, I came to understand at least some aspects of how the universe works. The universe is infinite, and I do not claim to know all the truth. Whether knowing everything about the universe is possible or not, I still have a curiosity to seek the full truth.

I discovered that we are not dropped on this Earth randomly. Our soul is part of source energy, powerful and independent, and it plans our life before coming to Earth. With the help of spirit guides, we decide our parents, siblings, place of birth, romantic partners, children, career, and important people in our life, according to our soul's evolution journey and the lessons we need to learn in certain lifetimes. We also have soul contracts with other souls.

Part of the plan involves us forgetting who we are so we can rediscover ourselves by evolving in physical form. While we may forget our powers and identity, we are never alone, as we are always connected to the source, spirit guides, and angels.

Spirit guides are advanced, evolved souls, or they can be our departed loved ones, spiritual masters who have left their bodies, or souls who have evolved to the fourth, fifth, sixth, and seventh planes. Our spirit guides help us navigate our life journey. Certain spirit guides assist us throughout our life, while others come to help during specific situations.

We also have a guardian angel who is always with us, never leaving us alone for a single moment. Our guardian angel loves us unconditionally and comforts us by sending the energy of unconditional love. There are many kinds of angels around us, whom we can ask for help and guidance.

Although we plan our lives with the help of our guides, source, and angels, we still have free will to make different decisions and choose different paths from our lower selves. The lower self consists of our physical self, mind, ego, and emotional self, while the higher self is our soul. We can even terminate soul contracts with other souls.

When we make choices different from our soul's plans, our soul does not judge us. Instead, it re-navigates our life journey to align with our soul's purpose in this lifetime. When we go off track, our life seems to stop working, and we feel overwhelmed, lost, and burnt out.

This happened with my friends Rohan and Iram. I knew intuitively and through Rajni's visions that they had a calling for awakening and healing in this lifetime, but their lower selves chose not to heal and got stuck in their ego. Just because Rajni and I listened to our calling and started working on ourselves does not mean we are better than them. They were simply not ready, but at any moment, their ego could surrender from exhaustion, allowing their souls to re-navigate them to the path of healing and awakening.

Rajni told me that Rohan and Iram are surrounded by their guides and angels, who are holding light for them and helping them navigate their lives.

God, spirit guides, and angels respect our free will, as one of the laws of the universe is free will. My life started changing when I gave permission to God, my spirit guides, and angels to help me. One of the affirmations that helped me is from Christina Lopes: "Dear God, spirit guides, and angels, I give you full permission to intervene in my life whenever you see fit." Another affirmation I use is, "Dear God, angels, and spirit guides, I give you full permission to help me whenever and wherever I need."

Help does not mean they will make our life easy all the time. Help means that when we are stuck because of our ego mind and struggling unnecessarily, they will show us the way to see things from a broader perspective. They can help us see our blind spots, bring the right people, situations, and circumstances into our lives so we can learn our lessons and grow. If we do not learn our lessons, the universe will keep sending the same types of people, situations, and circumstances over and over again until we learn.

If you have faith and believe, angels can help you in day-to-day life, like finding the right career, the right house, or lost keys and items. I have witnessed this myself; whenever I forget where I put my keys or anything else, I ask the angels to help me find them, then let it go. I receive an intuition about where the item is and find it easily.

Living in 3D reality as a human in a physical body is not easy, with so much darkness, negativity, and limitations. However, we are greatly loved and guided. If we open ourselves to receive guidance and help, our life can flow with more ease and abundance.

Help from guides and angels does not mean they will rescue us or that we won't have to go through our own hardships to learn lessons. We are powerful divine beings, and we must go through our self-discovery journey, healing, and inner transformation by ourselves. They can help us come into our personal power, but they cannot give our power back to us. We must claim our power and find our light within, as we always have this light within us, but we forget who we are.

From my and Rajni's self-discovery journeys, I have learnt that we are always guided. However, that help and guidance can come in many shapes and forms, according to our soul's essence, gifts, and talents.

Spirit Guides and Angels

Spirit guides and angels can communicate with some people while they are awake. Sometimes, they appear and communicate during deep meditation, or they communicate through direct downloads, feelings, and thoughts. Direct downloads are when the source or guides send information directly into our heads. Intuition occurs when our soul sends information to our heart, which then transmits it to our mind, and our mind processes and tells us this information.

My friend Rajni is gifted in communicating with and seeing guides, angels, and masters during her deep meditation. Once, she was trying to connect with Archangel Michael, and another angel appeared in her meditation. That angel told Rajni her name and informed her that Rajni did not yet have the contract to see and communicate with Archangel Michael.

Rajni has seen and communicated with several angels and guides in her meditation. She has seen Jesus, Baba Guru Nanak, and Shiva. Although they did not speak, Rajni said she felt immense unconditional love and an upgrade in her vibrations after feeling their presence. Up to the time of writing this book, she has had contact with one Blue Ray starseed, who gave Rajni information about the evolution of everything on this planet and how everything is evolving rapidly at this time in history.

I receive guidance through direct downloads, intuition, feelings, and sometimes thoughts. After meditating for many years and calming my mind, I am learning to differentiate between my own thoughts, other people's thoughts, and thoughts given by the source and guides. The insights I receive for my blind spots and blind spots of others are through direct downloads from my spirit guides and source.

I remind myself daily that I am loved and guided by saying an affirmation from Christina Lopes: "I am so loved and guided in everything I do, and so it is. I open my energy to receive answers and guidance."

Some people fear that if they open themselves to the spirit realm, they might encounter ghosts or evil spirits. The truth is, there is nothing to be afraid of. There are dark beings in the spirit realm, but they have no power over us and cannot harm us unless we allow them to. They feed on fear, and if we tell them to go away without fear, they will leave and never return.

In the beginning of our spiritual awakening, Rajni and I felt the presence of dark beings. Without feeling fear, we told them to go away, as they were not welcome. They never returned, and since then, we have only been visited by high-vibrational beings.

Although I have been guided throughout my life journey, becoming aware of this guidance has lifted the unnecessary burden I was carrying on my shoulders. My mind has started letting go of the need to control every move of my life. I have learned to live in the present moment, trusting that my soul knows where I am going and that I will follow my soul and guides without resistance.

The more we declutter our minds and open ourselves, the more insights, intuition, downloads, and guidance we will receive. Knowing that we are loved and guided, which we truly are, is comforting and can alleviate feelings of loneliness and abandonment. The truth is, we are never lonely and never abandoned. We are all guided.

www.ingramcontent.com/pod-product-compliance
Lightning Source LLC
Chambersburg PA
CBHW051521120626
46551CB00012B/1026